I was delighted to hear so many aspects of humming, crucially important for all human being's vocal activities, woven into the story so ably!

Introducing this story to our small listeners can have profound importance to them, as humming comes from unimaginable depths of our evolutionary prehistory, originating millions of years earlier than our speech. Deeper evolutionary roots naturally mean a more effective connection to human emotional life.

- Joseph Jordania, evolutionary musicologist, author of New Model of Human Evolution: How Predators Shaped Human Morphology and Behaviour. University of Melbourne, Australia .

***

This delightful book is fun for all ages—my 4-year-old granddaughter watched and listened all the way through and then went dancing and humming around the house.
"Grandma, I did like the book"
https://youtu.be/bwjYJHsWluk

As this book is being published, we are in tough times. This little story reminds us that we are all special and inspires us with both the beauty of nature in the artwork and the beauty of the human voice. As we preserve art, music, and especially beauty, humans will become a less destructive species.

- Marilyn Manzer, music educator,
  Wolfville, Nova Scotia

HARP: The People's Press

216 Clydesdale Road

Clydesdale, Nova Scotia

Canada B2G 2K9

www.harppublishing.ca

Information about purchasing copies of this book can be obtained from the publishers.

harppeoplespress@gmail.com

tel# 902.863.0396

Library and Archives Canada Cataloguing in Publication

ISBN: 978-0-9938295-7-4

Botanical Collages by Dorothy Lander

Digital Design by Cathy Lin

A Humming Primer

Hmmm was inspired by Nova Scotia writer Sheree Fitch who led a workshop for Arts Health Antigonish (AHA! – www.artshealthantigonish.org.) She invited us to choose a letter of the alphabet and write a poem or a story around it. I chose the letter M.

My original idea was simply to shape a story in which M, communicating entirely by humming, sought out the company of Nature's hummers—bees, hummingbirds, and dragonflies—to become an advocate for children and grown-ups who were different. I imagined M inviting them to commune with Nature. Inviting them to hum.

I knew instinctively that humming heals. The mother who hums her crying baby to sleep. Or the other end of the life span, humming a childhood song can be comforting and put elderly people in a good mood, especially if they know their memory is failing. It turns out a large body of research confirms the benefits of humming.

The benefits of humming on high blood pressure, elevated heart rate, depression, and sleep disturbances are well established. Humming has been shown to counter a sense of loneliness, and can reduce anxiety. Humming stimulates the sleep hormone, and can give us a blissful night's sleep. Humming may release tension held in the stomach, leading to a soft, relaxed belly, instead of one churning with anxiety.

These benefits have caught the attention of professional singers and competitive divers. When we hum with our mouth closed, vibrations are generated in our head. These vibrations shake up and thus break the bond of mucus and other secretions trapped in our sinuses, throat, nose and chest. If professionals hum as a way to recover from hoarseness or sore throat or laryngitis, it follows that it will have similar positive effects for those of us who sing and swim for pleasure.

We are hard-wired for humming. Ethnomusicologist Joseph Jordania traces the millions of years of its evolutionary purpose: from the survival of animal groups against predators to the safety and psychological comfort among human groups. Animal contact calls—like chicken clucks and horse neighs—signal that they are among kin, that there are no predators around, and that they can continue with the business at hand, like playing or eating. The absence of sound served as an alert to other animals to remain silent and look for the possible source of danger.

Today, human humming serves to convey secret knowledge in complex codes that can signal either that we can let down our guard and relax or we should go on full alert for danger. Think of Hmmmm's of approval or agreement with another's point of view, or as an expression of comfort.

Contrast these Hmmmm's to the complex coded language of humming that features in two unforgettable fictional characters, representing European and African-American cultures: Madame DeFarge in Charles Dickens' The Tale of Two Cities, set in the time of the French Revolution, and L, the hummer who opens and closes Toni Morrison's family history novel Love. set in America's Deep South. Madame DeFarge hummed over her knitting, and as the spy entered the Parisian wine-shop that she ran with her husband, she signalled with an 'accidental' touch of her elbow along with accelerated humming that Monsieur DeFarge would do "best to answer, but with brevity" (p. 184). In Love, L's hum, reminiscent of the practice of women slaves working side by side on plantations, conveys a deeper knowledge and a greater emotional range than voiced words. L hums to share sorrow and joy. L teaches companion humming to Heed and Christine to create a diversion and avoid brutal abuse. Such complex multi-purpose humming is part of our evolutionary history.

And so it was that M's story became a showcase for all different kinds of humming—soft and loud, happy and sad, tuneful and monotone. It invites readers to hum along with M whenever *Hm-mmm* appears in the story.

As a preamble to M's story, here are some basic pointers for your humming practice that will allow your vocal cords to resonate freely.

With your mouth closed, move your tongue and jaw to change the shape, and thus the resonance of your humming. Feel all those vibrations bouncing around in your head. When you feel the most vibrations in your face, your tongue and jaw are in the right position. If you are humming to recover from a sore throat or cold, you will want to feel the most vibrations in your forehead.

To get started:
Close your mouth and let the front part of the tongue rest in its natural place in the roof of the mouth, behind the front teeth.

Breathe out saying "*Hmmmm* ..." That is, push together your vocal cords to squeeze the air through the nose so that a humming sound occurs.

If you have a yoga meditation practice that includes the "om" chant, you already have a humming practice. Humming — or Brahmaree Pranayama, is a breathwork technique in yoga and Ayurveda. Brahmari means “the bee.” It relaxes the mind and the nervous system. Simply take a few slow, deep breaths through the nose with tightly sealed lips. Each time you breathe out, make a humming sound like a buzzing bee or wasp. Notice how the inner walls of your nostrils and voice box vibrate with the noise. See if the muscles in your face, jaws and shoulders are relaxing while you hum.

Why hum? In some of the happiest countries in the world, like Myanmar and Mexico, as determined by the Global Happiness Index, there is far more human noise than there is in North America and Europe—talking, shouting, singing, laughing and yes, humming.

Our exposure to social media and electronic devices means we spend much of our lives in vocal deserts especially if we spend long days in front of our computers or smart phones. We need to use our voice boxes to prevent some of the new health challenges of our wired world.

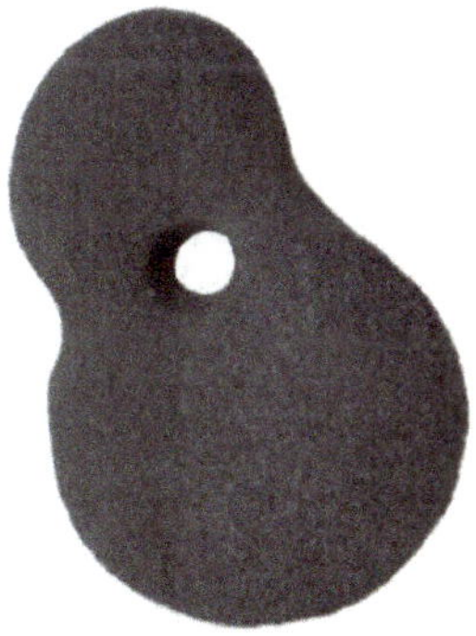

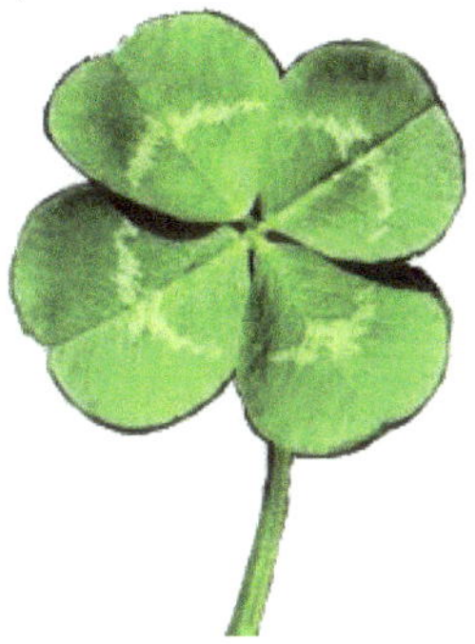

We invite you to hum along with M as you read or listen to her story. Hum for luck whenever you spy a four-leaf clover or an adder-stone.

Hum loud, hum soft, hum often. Hmmmm Hmmmm

Dorothy Lander, Clydesdale, Nova Scotia, 2019

Jordania, Joseph (2010). Music and Emotions: Humming in Human Prehistory . Available from http://symposium.polyphony.ge/wp-content/uploads/2016/04/02.Joseph-Jordania.eng_.pdf

Hmmmm

M the Humdinger

M was a hummer.

She came into the world humming. Her very first sounds were *Hmmmm Hmmmm*

She hummed when she was hungry. *Hmmmm*

She hummed when she was tired. *Hmmmm*

She hummed through breakfast, lunch and dinner.

Hmmmm Hmmmm Hmmmm

She hummed in her sleep. All night long.

Hmmmmmmmmmmmmmmmmmmmmmmmmmm...

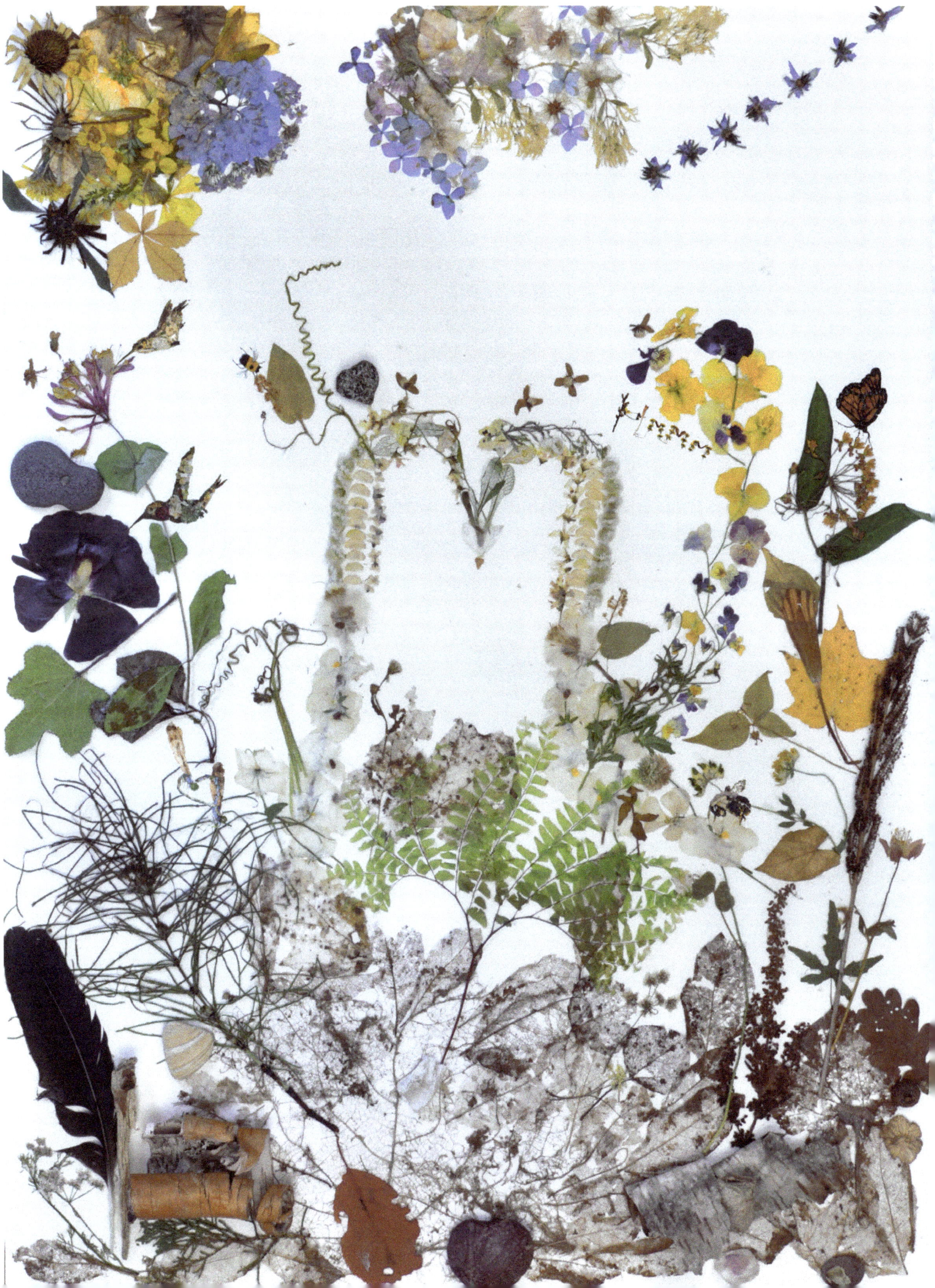

She loved to go outdoors into the flower garden. There she would find herself surrounded by all kinds of other hummers — bees, dragonflies, hummingbirds.

M liked to tuck herself right into the flowers and bask in an explosion of humming. She hummed call-and-response with all the other hummers.

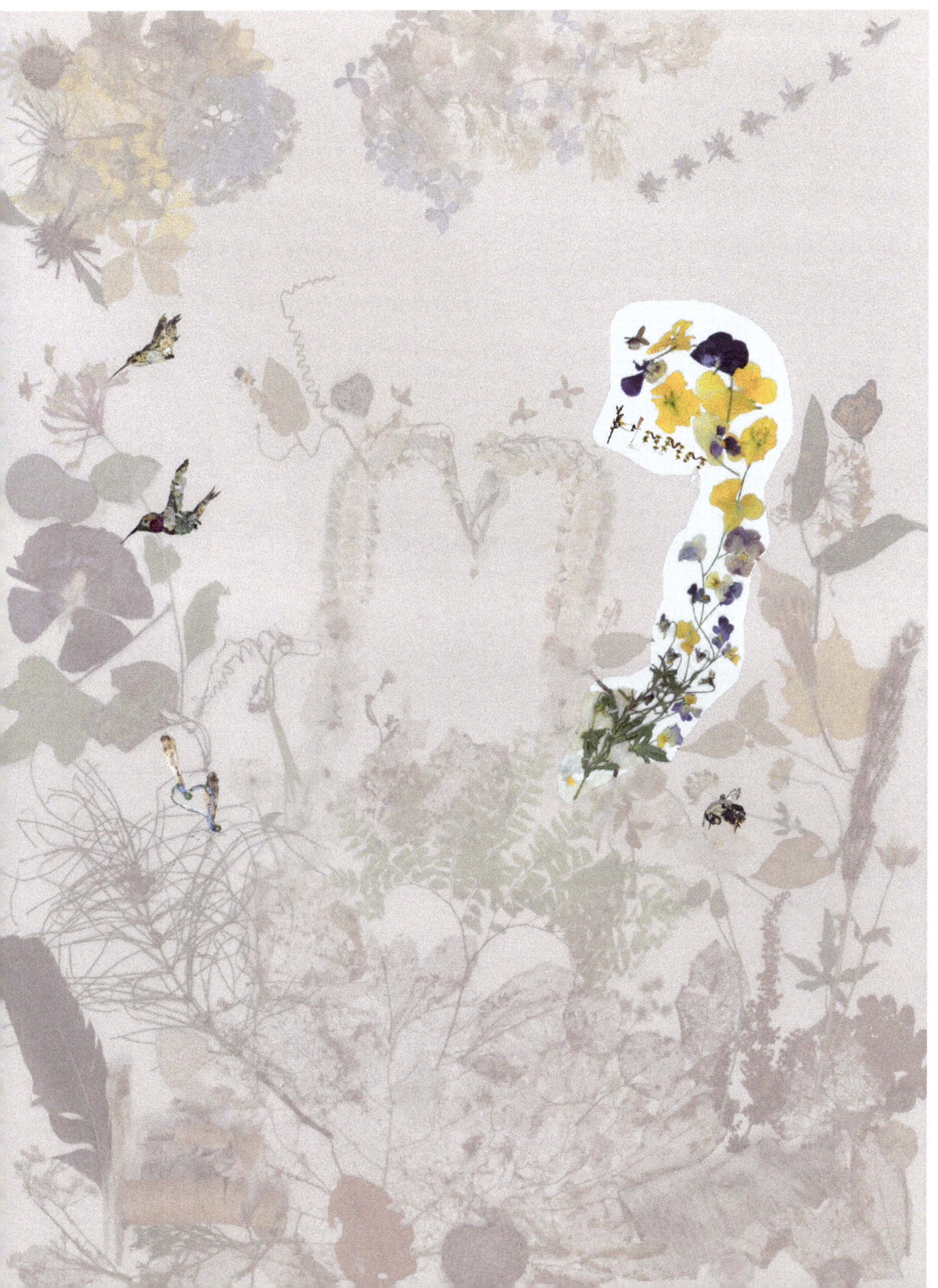

M did not come from a family of hummers. Her mother and father, sisters and brothers did not know what to make of her. How was it she was different from the rest of the family?

They begged her to stop. She could not.

They clapped their hands over their ears. They tried everything they could think of to get her to stop.

They squeezed her tight as tight could be.

Louder, breathless humming:

Hmmmm . . . ohmmmm . . . Hmmmm . . . ohmmmm

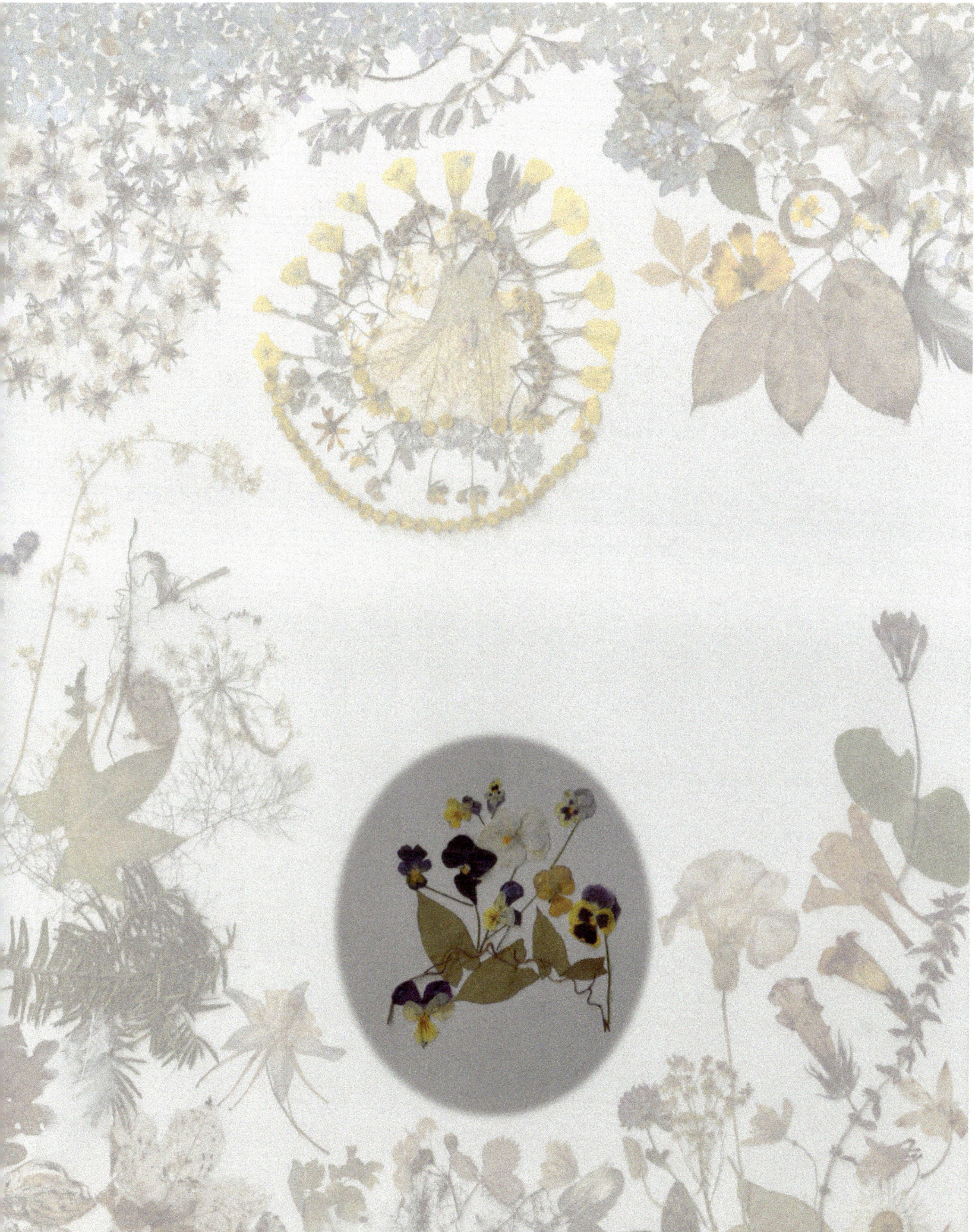

They scrunched their faces and stuck out their tongues.
M scrunched right back and kept on humming.

Hmmmm Hahmmmm . . . Hmmmm Hahmmmm

At first, M's mom and dad thought they would have to shelter her from the rest of the world.
She had no playmates except her sisters and brothers.
She kept on humming.

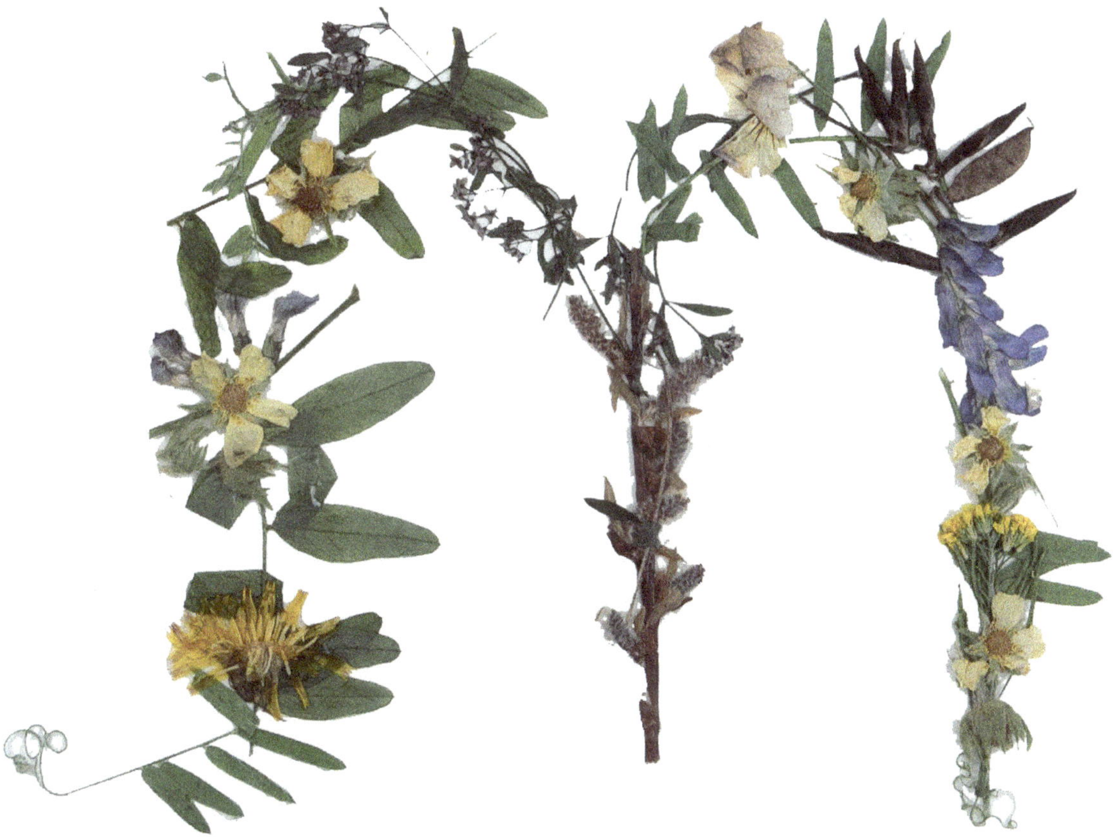

Then they tried mixing her with playmates of her own age. They marveled at the many different humming sounds and tunes M could make. But by and by they too tried to stop her humming.

They pushed her high in the sky on the swing. She hummed in rhythm with each back and forth.

Hmmmm . . . Hummmm

Hmmmm . . . Hummmm

Hmmmm . . . Hummmm

They popped the sweetest wild strawberries into M's mouth. She smacked her lips, savoured the little heart-berries, and kept on humming.

Hmmmm Yummmmmm . . .

Hmmmm Yummmmmm . . .

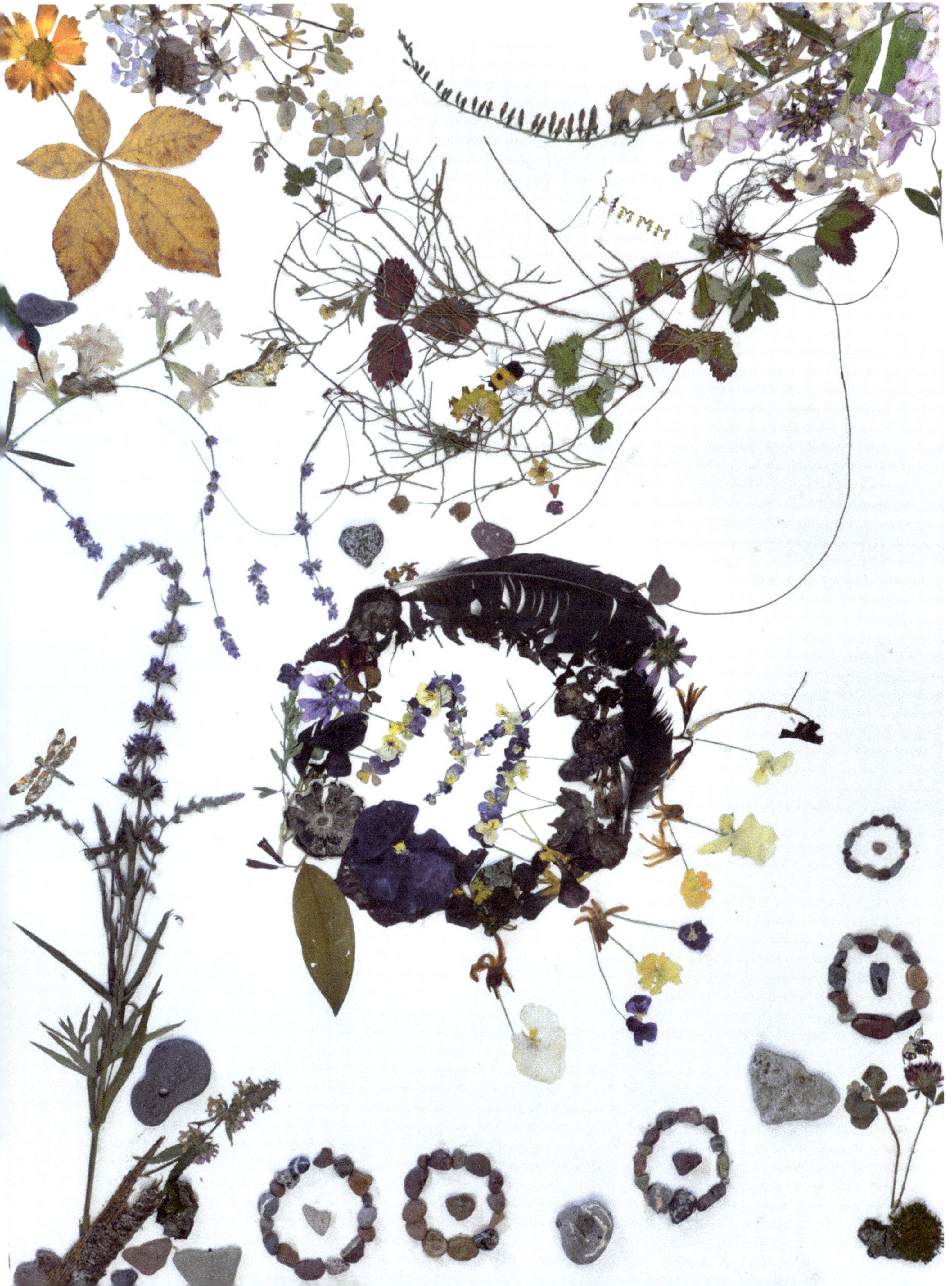

They sprinkled the strongest scented lavender buds over M's head. She beamed and kept on humming.

Hmmmm Hmmmm Hmmmm

They kissed her on the cheeks and in the middle of her forehead. Sibilant humming.

Ssshmmm Ssshmmm Ssshmmm

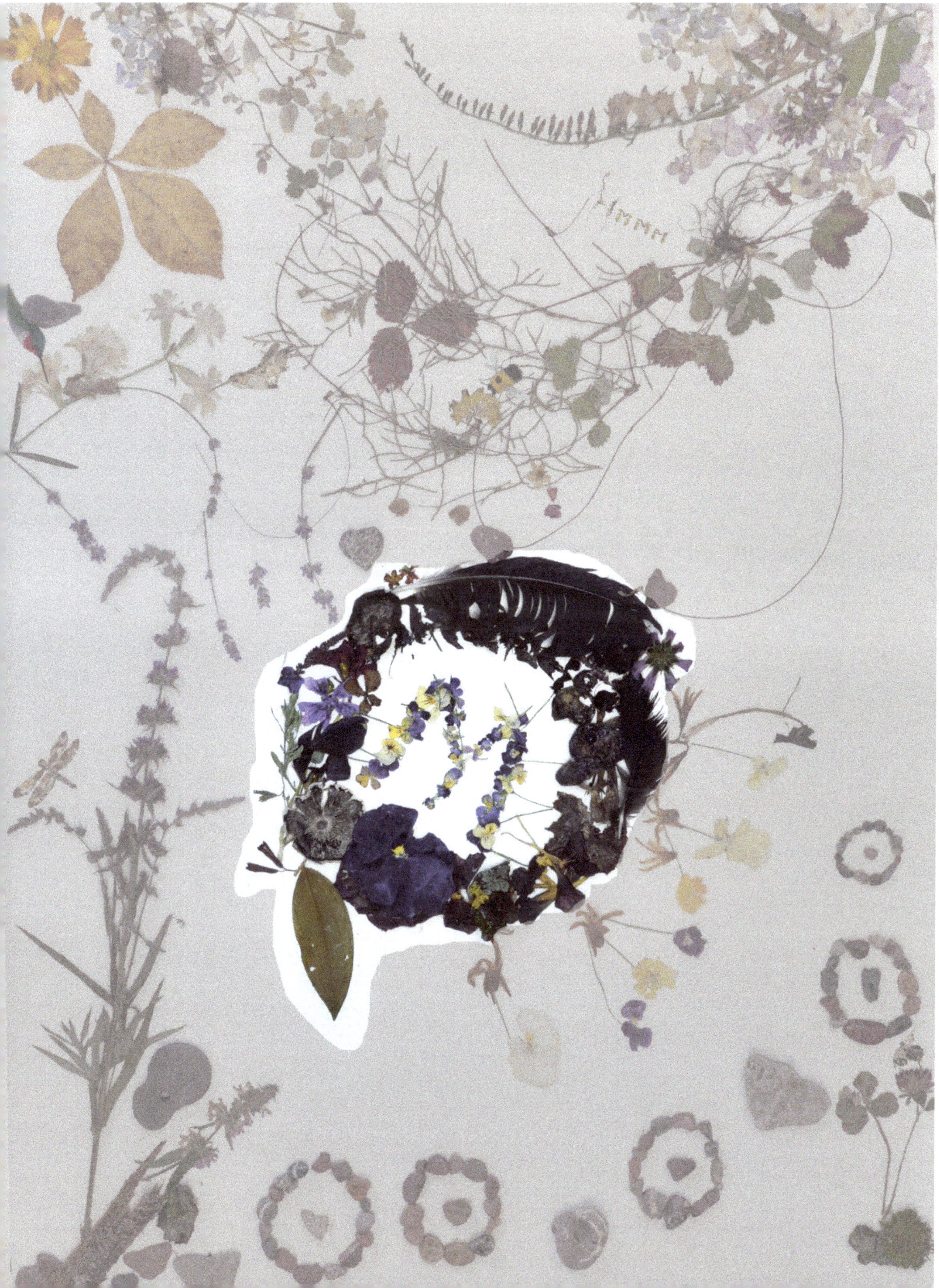

Soon M's siblings and playmates came to love playing with M. Every kind of play was a hum-along, in which M invented a new melody to accompany their adventures. Whenever her friends or siblings had a birthday party, M would hum along as everyone sang Happy Birthday. But then she would do something extra. She would hum a new tune that was special for the birthday girl or boy.

Hummmmmmmmmmmmmmmmmmmmmmmmmmmmm

Everyone would gather in close to M to be part of her special circle. It was at one of these birthday parties that someone began to chant: "M's a humdinger. M's a humdinger." Everyone joined in and so it became part of every celebration that M honoured with a humming tribute.

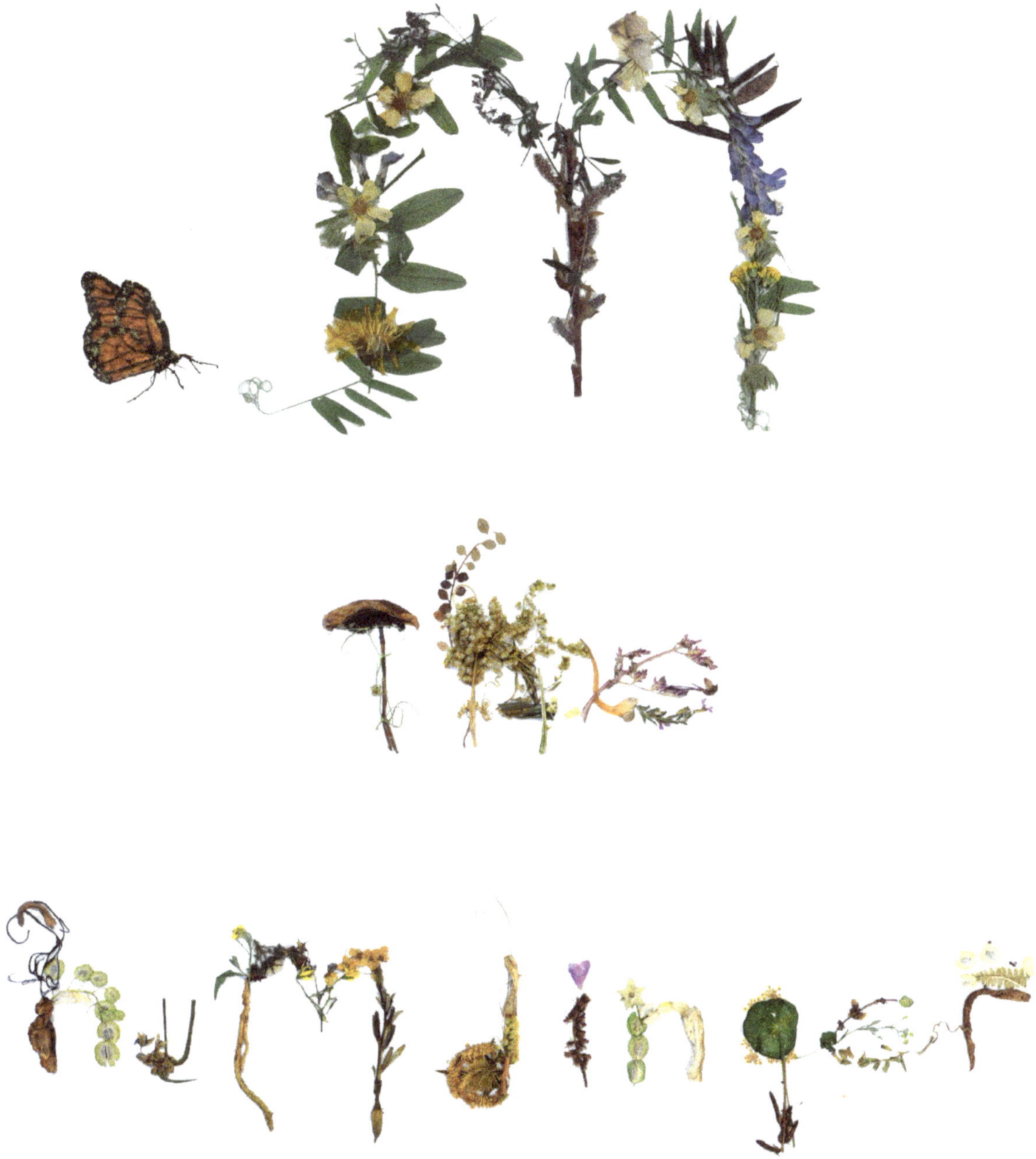
the
humdinger

Mom and Dad were not so sure this happiness would last when M got older and started school. Would she be excluded, even bullied, because of being different?

They wondered if M's humming could be a physical ailment. Perhaps there was a blockage in her throat? They took her to a children's doctor — a pediatrician. She examined M from tip to toe. She felt M's wrist with her two middle fingers and took her pulse. "90 beats per minute. Perfect." Then she put her ear to M's chest and listened to her heart beat. "Lub-dub. Lub-dub. Lub-dub. Very regular, M."

The doctor helped M put her stethoscope into her own ears to listen, then couldn't help laughing as M then proceeded to hum her own heartbeat:

Lubmmmmm – Dubmmmmmm

Lubmmmmm – Dubmmmmmm.

The doctor then asked M to open her mouth wide and hum as loudly as she could.

HMMMMMMMMMMMMMMMM

"Nothing out of order," said the doctor. "Your little girl is the picture of health. But just in case I have missed something, I will refer you to a specialist — the ear, nose, and throat doctor. ENT for short." And with that she made her notes and began a file on M.

Mom and Dad took M to the ENT doctor. She took her laser light and peered into M's ears, then her nose, then her throat. She asked her to open her mouth and hum as loudly as she could.

HMMMMMMMMMMMMMM

Then she asked M to hum as softly as she could.

hmmmmmmmmmmmmmmmmmmmmmmmmmmm

Then she asked M to hum a favourite tune. M began to hum Beethoven's 5th Symphony.

Hmmm

Hmmm

Hmmm

Hmmm

Hmmmmm

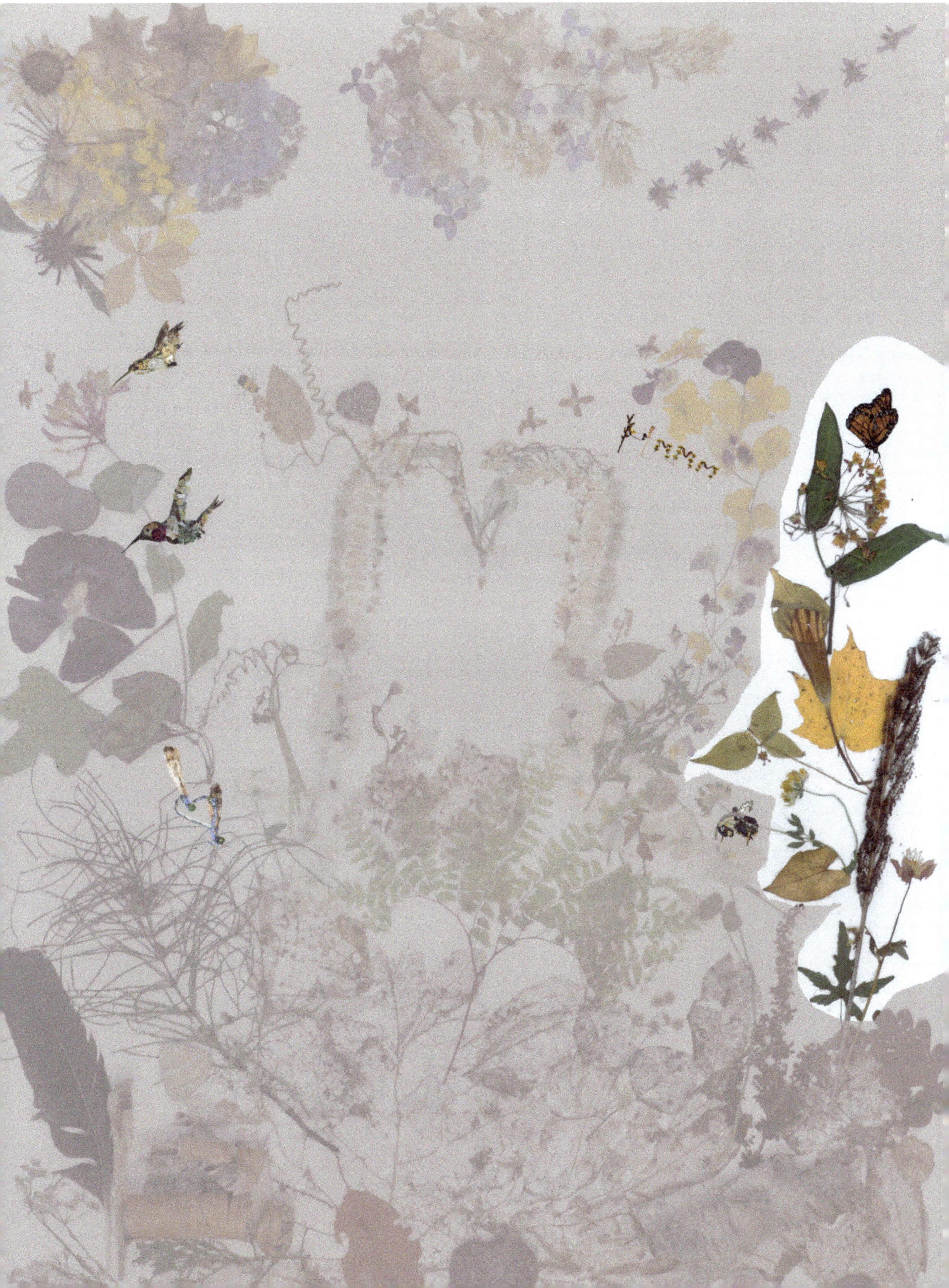

The doctor listened with wonderment. "Your little girl is the picture of health. She has the most exquisite vocal cords I have ever examined in a child. Already, her vocal cords are above the average of 23 millimetres long. I have only one piece of advice. I see a lot of singers and actors in my practice. Our vocal cords are composed of very sensitive pliable soft tissue, and need to be constantly hydrated to keep it that way."

Turning to M, "Do try to drink as much water and other drinks as you can — but try to avoid sugary drinks like pop. And when you are older, avoid tea or coffee, because this can dry you out. Here is an easy check. Your pee should be a pale yellow." Mom and Dad nodded, and M hummed that she understood.

Hmmmm

Finally, the doctor said, "Just in case I have missed something, say an early trauma, I will refer M to a child psychologist." And with that, the doctor made her notes and began a file on M.

Mom and Dad took M to the psychologist. He asked M to hum different emotions.

"M, can you hum happy?"

Hm hmmm hm hmmm hm hmmm

"M, can you hum sad?"

hm oochmmmm hm oochmmm hmoochmm ooochmmm

"M, can you hum angry?"

M gritted her teeth and hummed:

HMMMMMMMMMMnnnnnnnnnnn

“M, can you hum fear?”

hmm hmm hmm hmm hmm hmm

The psychologist spoke with confidence. “Your little girl is the picture of emotional health. She can express a psychological range far beyond her years.” And with that, the doctor made his notes and began a file on M.

Mom and Dad felt reassured, but in case conventional medicine had missed something, they sought out a naturopathic doctor. The doctor asked M if she could prick her finger gently to gather just a drop of blood. M had become trusting of doctors and hummed her assent.

Hmm Hmm.

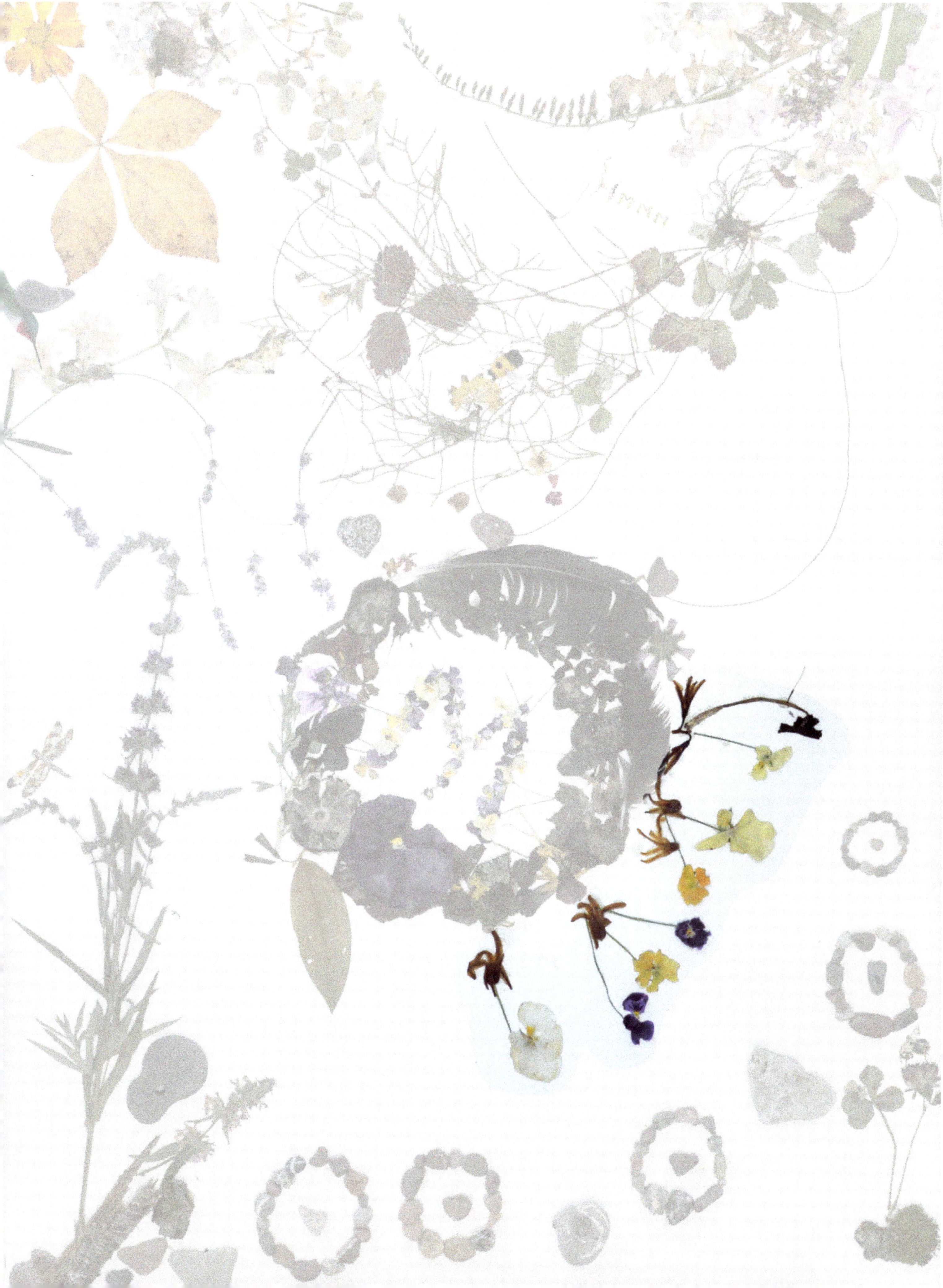

She then looked at M's blood under the microscope to see how healthy her cells looked.

Mom and Dad and M looked at the red and white blood cells dancing on the screen. The doctor marveled at how round and smooth M's cells were. She spoke. "Beautiful cells. M, you are the picture of health. And you have a great gift." Turning to M's Mom and Dad, she said, "M is not a Special Needs child. She is a Special Gifts child." And with that, she made her notes and began a file on M.

Just as they were leaving, the naturopath said, "There is no pill or potion to stop M humming. This is not a health issue. For extraordinary gifts like M's, I recommend you visit the Wise Woman. She lives in a tiny hut deep in the forest glen known as the Valley of the Big Stone, which is surrounded by magnificent oaks. She knows about gifts of body, mind, and spirit.

Mom and Dad and M walked deep into the ravine to the mouth of the spring and found the Wise Woman sitting on the black granite stone, cushioned with thick green moss. She was busy bundling dried herbs and medicinal plants—hyssop, fireweed, and wild cucumber—and arranging freshly gathered mushrooms on spruce boughs. The dwarf white roses (Rosa blanda) were blooming, and several kinds of vetches—purple, white, and penciled—were twining among the grass. The scent of roses filled the air, as did the loud hum of bees and dragonflies. The bees were vibrating their wings at the natural frequency of the pollen grains, releasing them from the anthers. M's humming riff immediately picked up on the bees' different foraging frequencies as they moved from bloom to bloom.

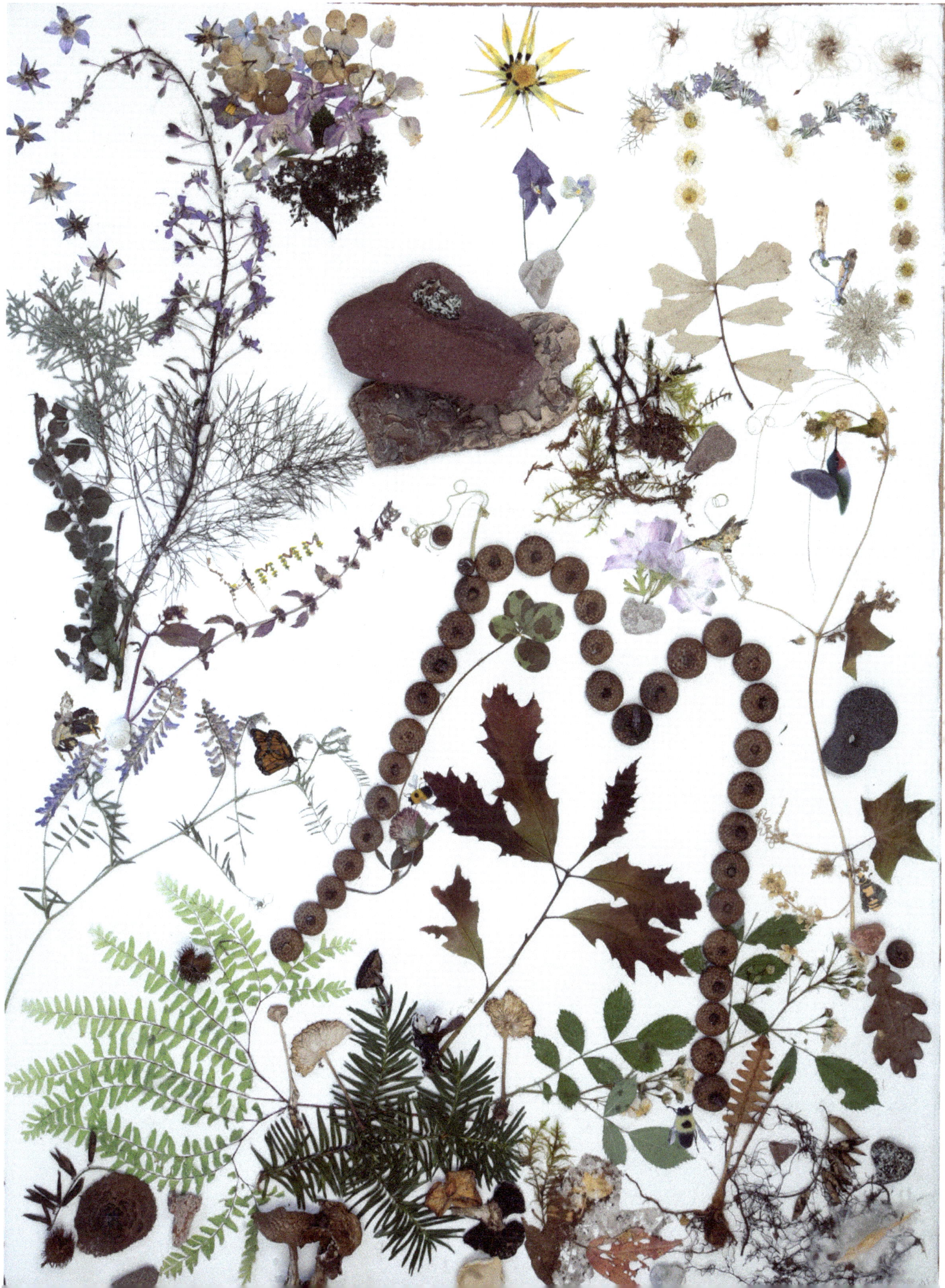

When Mom and Dad told her why they were visiting her, the Wise Woman asked if they would leave her alone with M and come back before the sun reached its highest point. M and the Wise Woman sat cross-legged on the cushion of moss facing each other across the Big Stone. The Wise Woman did not speak. She did not ask M any questions. She simply fixed her eyes on M's and listened intently as M hummed.

Hmmm Hymn Hmmmmmm Hymnnnn hmmmm hymnnnnnn HMMMMMMM HYM-MMNNN

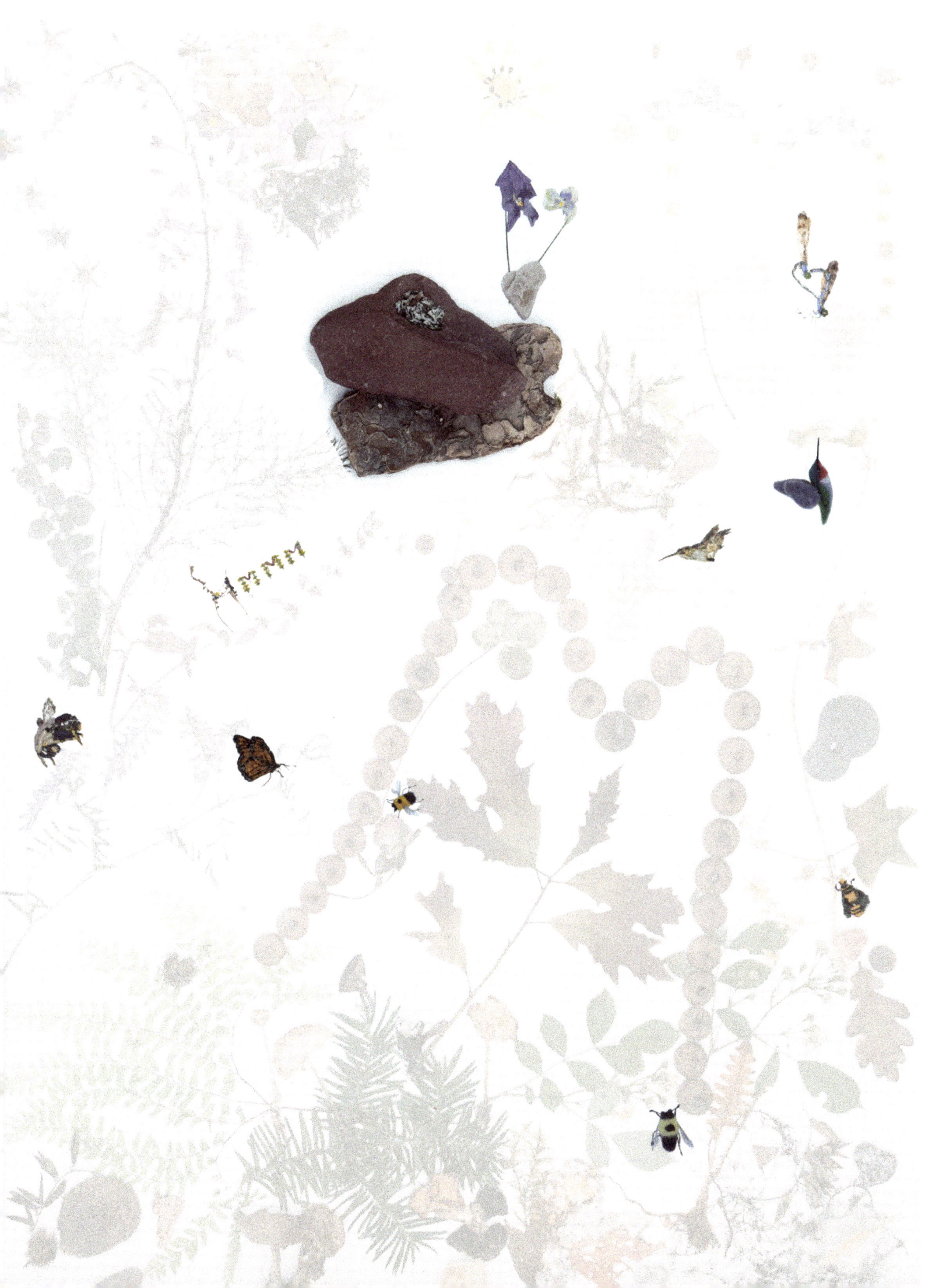
HMMM

M had never experienced such perfect attention to her humming. She felt the glow of love as if she were the most special being in the universe. She hummed with abandon and presented the whole range of her humming repertoire to her attentive elder. Occasionally, the Wise Woman would nod or smile.

It seemed as if no time had passed before Mom and Dad returned. Only then did the Wise Woman speak.

She addressed her words to M. "M, you will always belong to your family and friends. But first you belong to Nature." And with that she led M back through the oaks and firs to the edge of the forest. She guided her right into the middle of a honeysuckle bush in full bloom. There M was encircled by a throng of ruby-throated hummingbirds. Instantly, M began to hum in harmony with her bird companions.

Hmmmmmm Mmmmmm ...

Hmmmmmm Mmmmmm ...

By and by, M and the humming birds were joined by a swarm of honey bees. They did not sting M even once. Instead, the humming in the honeysuckle took on the beauty and complexity of a full symphony orchestra. The humming birds took up the string sections.
The bees were both the drum section and the reeds.

M happily hummed all the other parts.

Hmmmmm Hymnnnn Mmmmm ...

Hmmmmm Hymnnnn Mmmmm ...

Everyday M's family and playmates checked on her. With each passing day, they found M humming deeper and deeper into the honeysuckle.

HmmmM HmmmM ... HmmmM HmmmM

M's playmates were drawn to the honeysuckle and chose it as a favourite place to dance and play. Especially circle games. It was a joyous time. Here we go round the Mulberry Bush turned into Here we go Round the Honeysuckle Bush.

Oh My

Everyone was looking for ways to play out how much they had learned from M about love and friendship between people who are different. So together they invented a humming circle game to play around the honeysuckle bush. They numbered off as either honey-suckle, which spirals counterclockwise towards the sun, or morning glory, which coils clockwise to the sun. M invented a humming melody and every time the humming changed direction, the players swung their partner.

Hmmmmmmmmmmmm Hmmmmmmmmmmmm

As the humming came to an end, every honeysuckle and morning glory sought the other to fold in a hug.

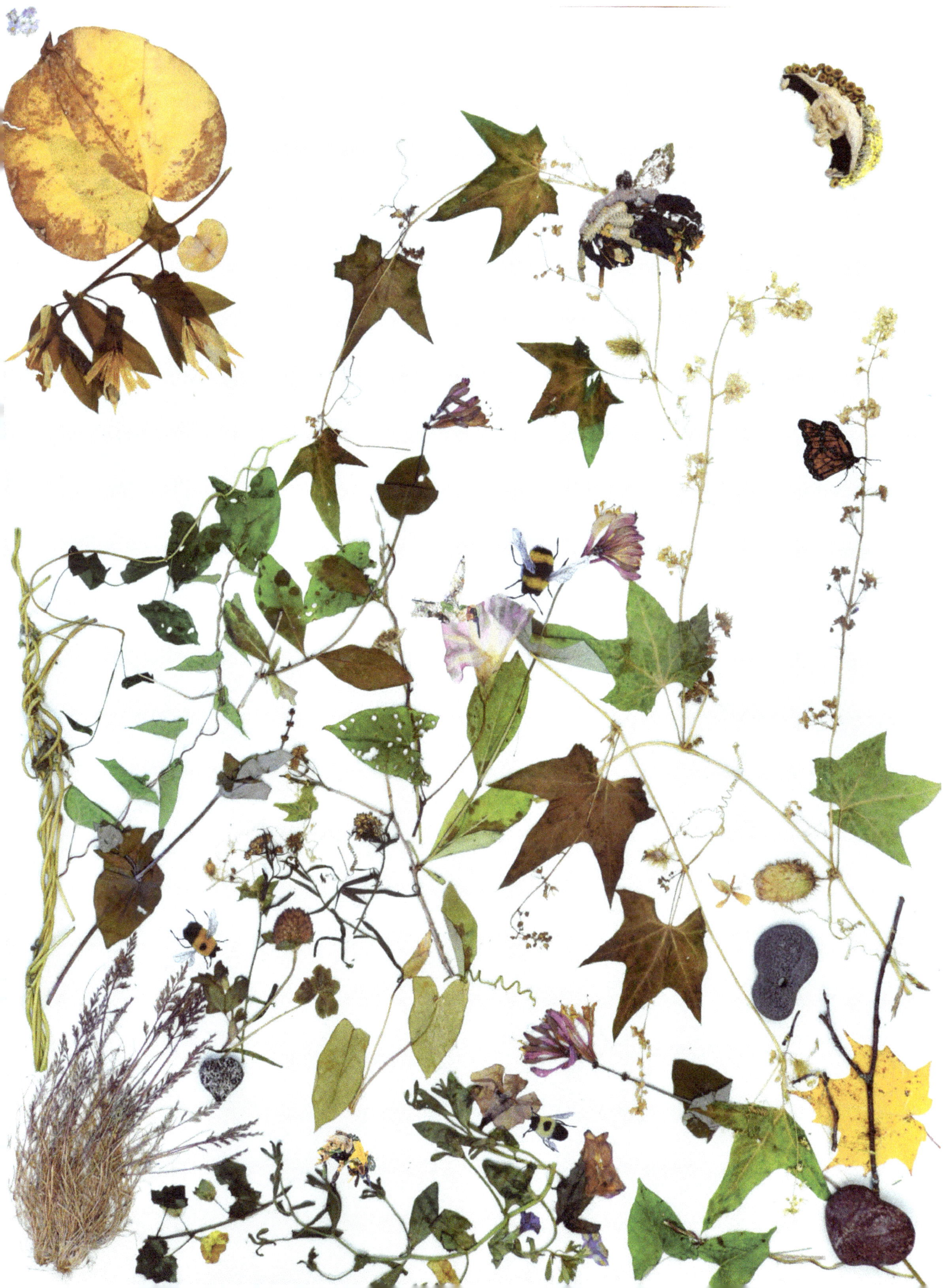

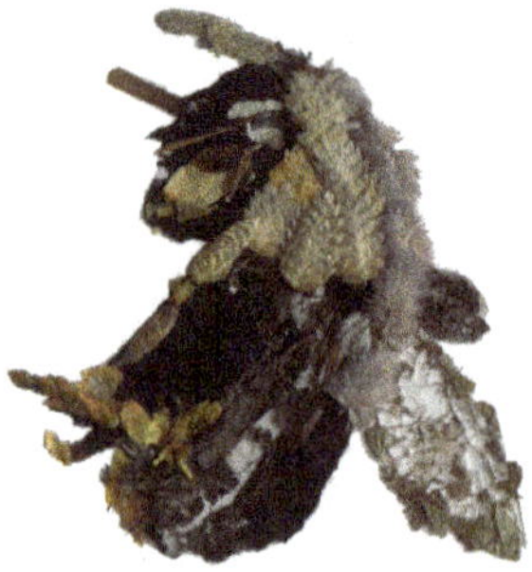

Humble Bumble

Hummed to the Sun

Humble Bumble

Thrummed to the Moon

Humble Bumble Humdinger

Hmmmm Hmnnnn

Humble Bumble tumbled on a morning glory

Humdinger left

Hmmmm Hmnnnn

Humble Bumble rumbled on a honeysuckle

Humdinger right

Hnnnn Hnnnn

Humble Bumble stumbled on a wild cucumber

Humdinger left three times

Hmmm Hmmm Hmmm

Humdinger right three times

Hmnn Hmnn Hmnn

Humble Bumble twined with the vine

Humble Bumble hummed to the sun

Hmmm Hmnn . . . Hmmm Hmnn

Humble Bumble Humdinger.

M's family and friends felt a great peace come over them. This tranquil space of honouring our different ways of being was M's blessing. They continued to gather around the honeysuckle and fold themselves into the humming circle.

One day, M could no longer be found in the honey-suckle. As her family and playmates peered into the depths, the honeysuckle began to tremble and shake, and then to hum.

Hymmmmmmmmmmmmmmmmmmmmmmmmmmmmmmm

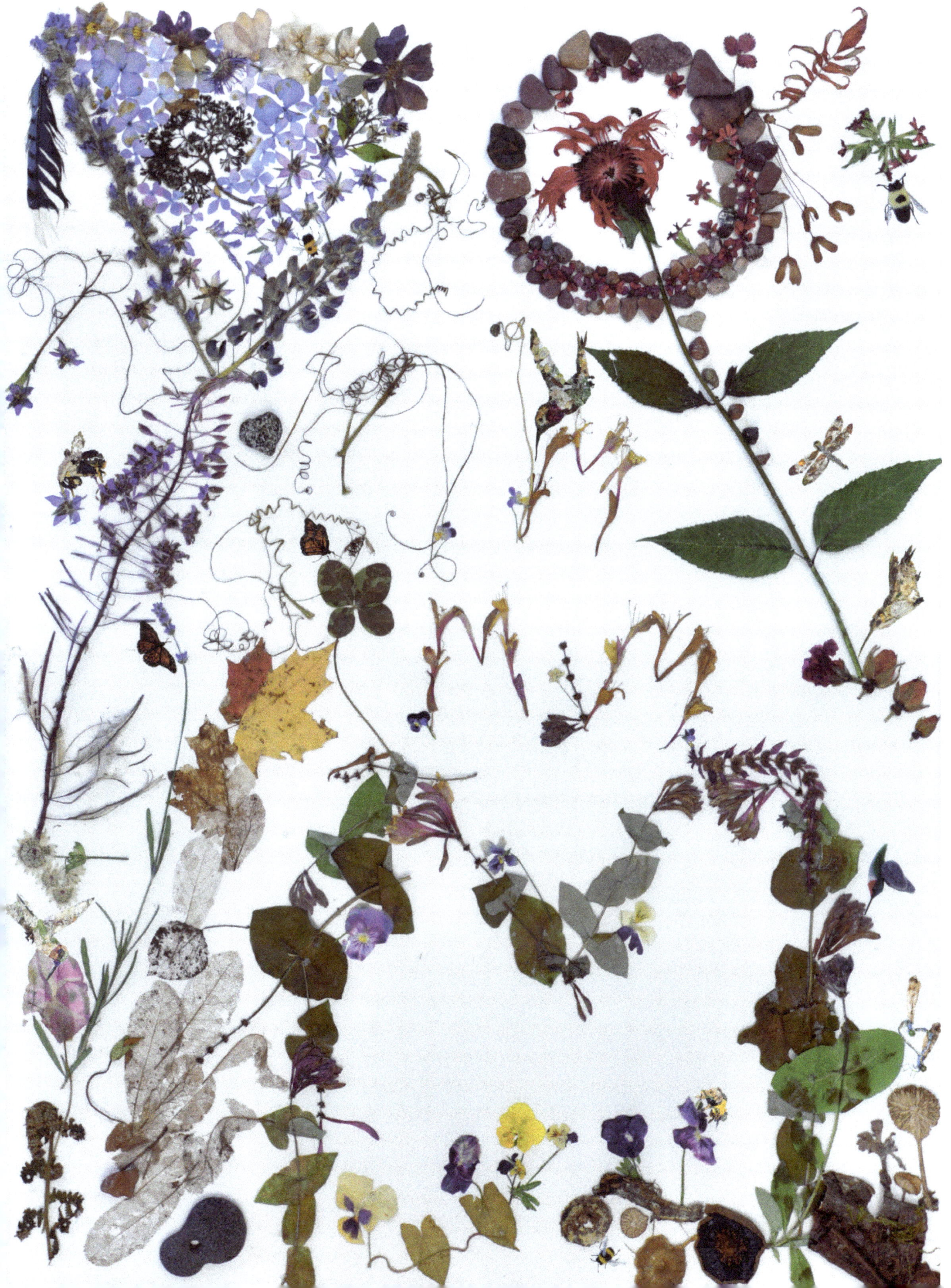
Mum

They began to notice when they played the Humdinger circle game that the honeysuckle tree was exuding the familiar *Hmmm* and *Hmnn* as the players swung their partners on each clockwise and counter-clockwise turn—and with the final embrace, they heard a harmonious and soft extended

Hmmmmmmmmmmmmnnnnnnnnnnnnnnnnn

Hmmm hymnnnn Mmmmmmmm

Hmmm hymnnnn mmmmmmmm …

And so it was until the end of time.

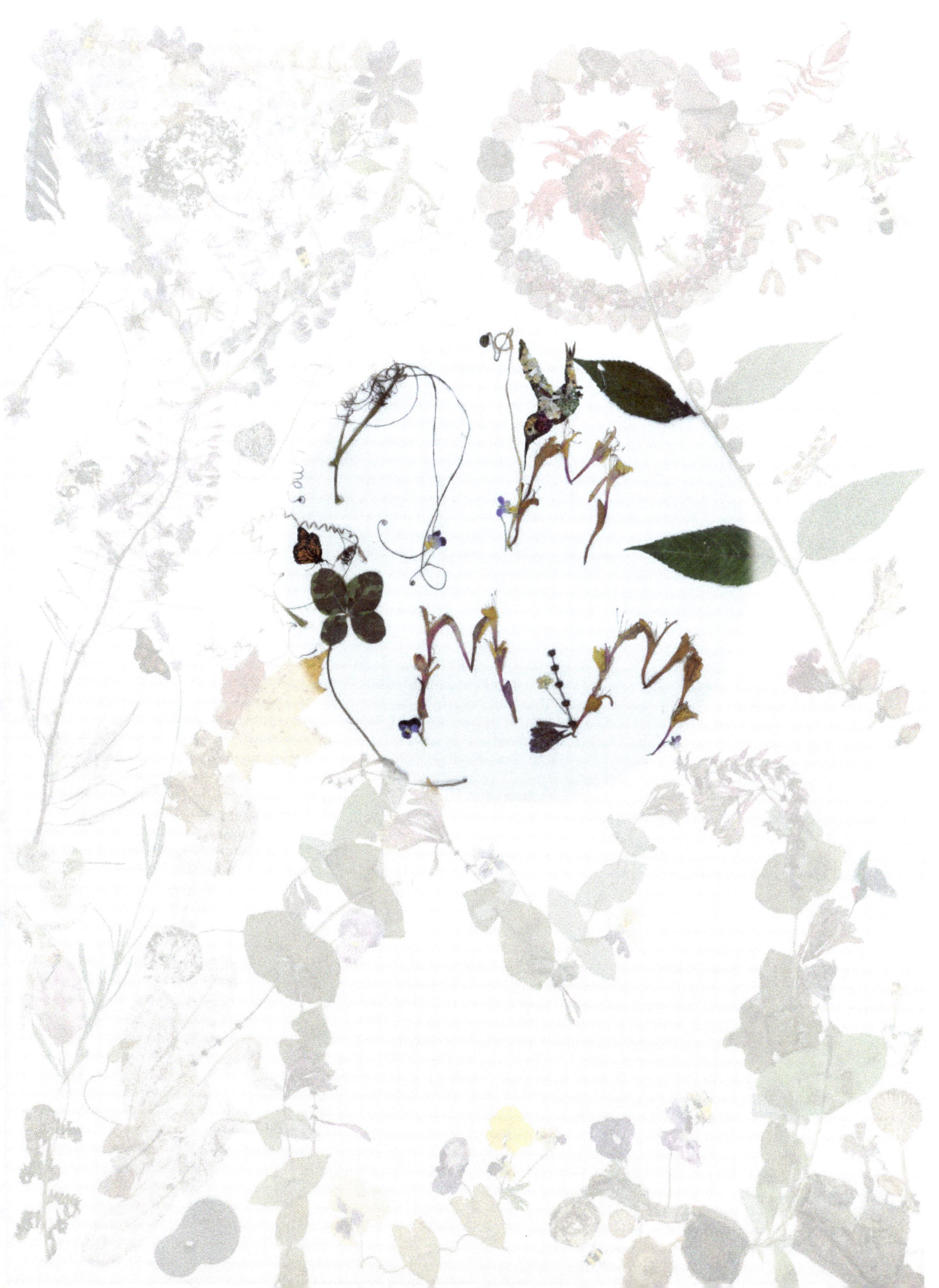
Oh Mum

Gratitude in Words and Images

Hmmm represents a collaboration that draws on the narrative vision and botanical collages of Dorothy Lander, the inspirational storyboard planning with Anne Camozzi and John Graham-Pole, the felted bees and hummingbirds of Nellie Fraser, the digital design talents of Cathy Lin, and above all, Nature's art in all its beauty and variation.

My gratitude to countless family and friends who contributed their bounty of flowers, moss and mycelium, leaves and evergreens, for the illustrations. In the early 1980s, my mother, as was her custom, enclosed with her handwritten letter the pressed columbine that appears on the front cover.

The Valley of the Big Stone and the plants that feature in the setting for the Wise Woman may strike a chord with students of Canadian women's history, children's literature and wildflowers. As a devotee of author and botanist Catharine Parr Traill, her 1852 children's story Lost in the Backwoods (later re-named Canadian Crusoes: A Tale of the Rice Lake Plains) held me in its grip from an early age. I grew up on the Rice Lake Plains and the Valley of the Big Stone was on our family farm known as Tower Farm. In the 1980s, my mother visiting me in Nova Scotia dug up and transported a dwarf white rose bush (rosa blanda) from the Valley of the Big Stone. Descendants of the rose bushes from the story of the three lost children appear in the plant collage illustrating M's visit with the Wise Woman.

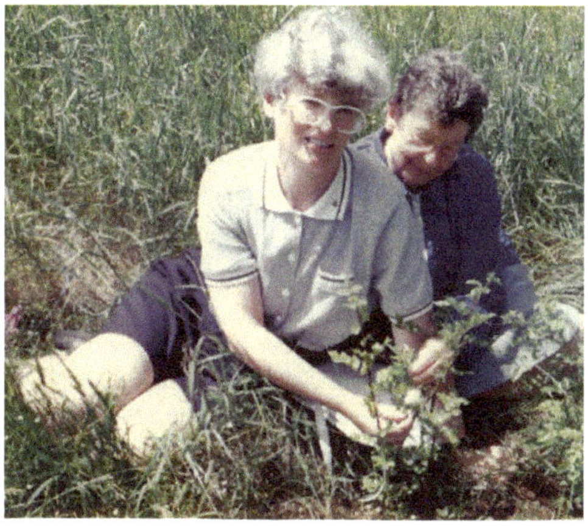

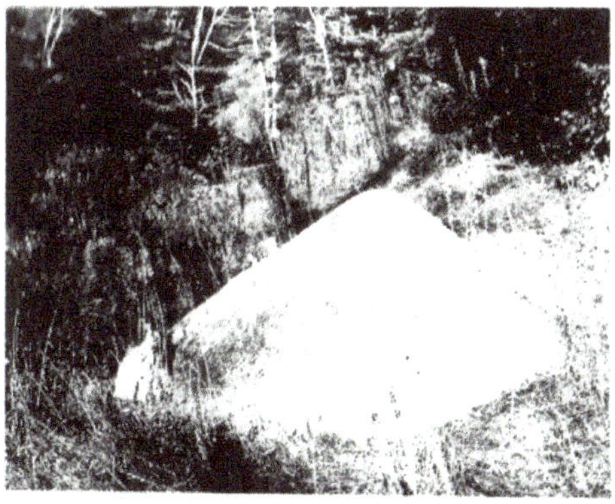

The granite boulder in Valley of the Big Stone, almost buried in silt

The Big Stone is now buried in silt as shown in the photo from the 1986 history of Gore's Landing and the Rice Lake Plains by Norma Martin, Catherine Milne and Donna S. McGillis.

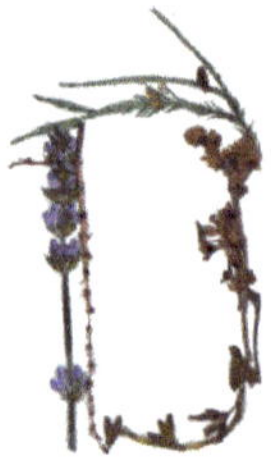

Dorothy chose the typeface Theano Didot as a close match to the D in her name. The prestigious history of the Didot typeface also had great appeal. Published in 1784 Paris by the famed Didot family of printers and type producers, its stylistic features of strong contrast, minimal embellishment, and mathematical precision, reflect the values of the Age of Enlightenment, the 18th-century people's revolution that rigorously questioned established institutions and aristocratic governance.

HARP The People's Press is committed to rigorous questioning of top-down leadership. And the first publication date of 1784 has deep resonance for HARP, our publishing house, based in Antigonish, Nova Scotia, where its first permanent European settlement was established in 1784.

Dorothy was delighted to discover the resource of the biggest online font library — pickafont.com — for the Honeybee and Dragonfly TrueType typefaces that form the Hmmm s.

A nod to Shakespeare (A Midsummer's Night Dream) and Flanders and Swan (Misalliance) for the inspiration of featuring bindweed and honeysuckle to represent the intertwining of difference.

Sleep thou, and I will wind thee in my arms.
Fairies, begone, and be all ways away.
So doth the woodbine the sweet honeysuckle
Gently entwist; the female ivy so
Enrings the barky fingers of the elm.
O, how I love thee! how I dote on thee!
~ AMND 4.1

The fragrant honeysuckle spirals clockwise to the sun,
And many other creepers do the same.
But some climb anti-clockwise, the bindweed does, for one,
Or Convolvulus, to give her proper name....
Each corkscrewed to the lintel in the only way it knew,
Where they stopped, touched tendrils, smiled, and fell in love.
~ Misalliance, Flanders and Swann

A round of applause to M's humming companions — bees, dragonflies, damselflies, and hummingbirds:

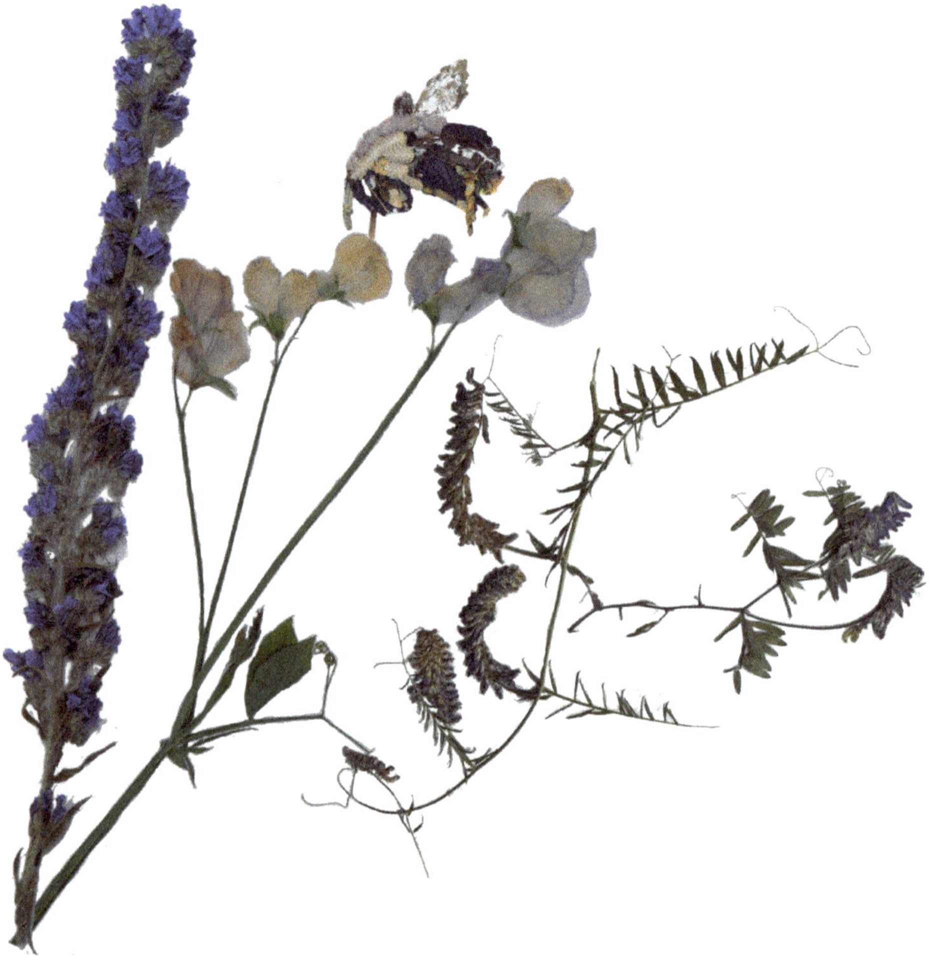

Bumble bee	- bombus impatiens
Tufted vetch	- vicia cracca
Viper's bugloss	- echium vulgare
Sweet pea	- lathyrus odoratus
Monarch butterfly	- danaus plexippus

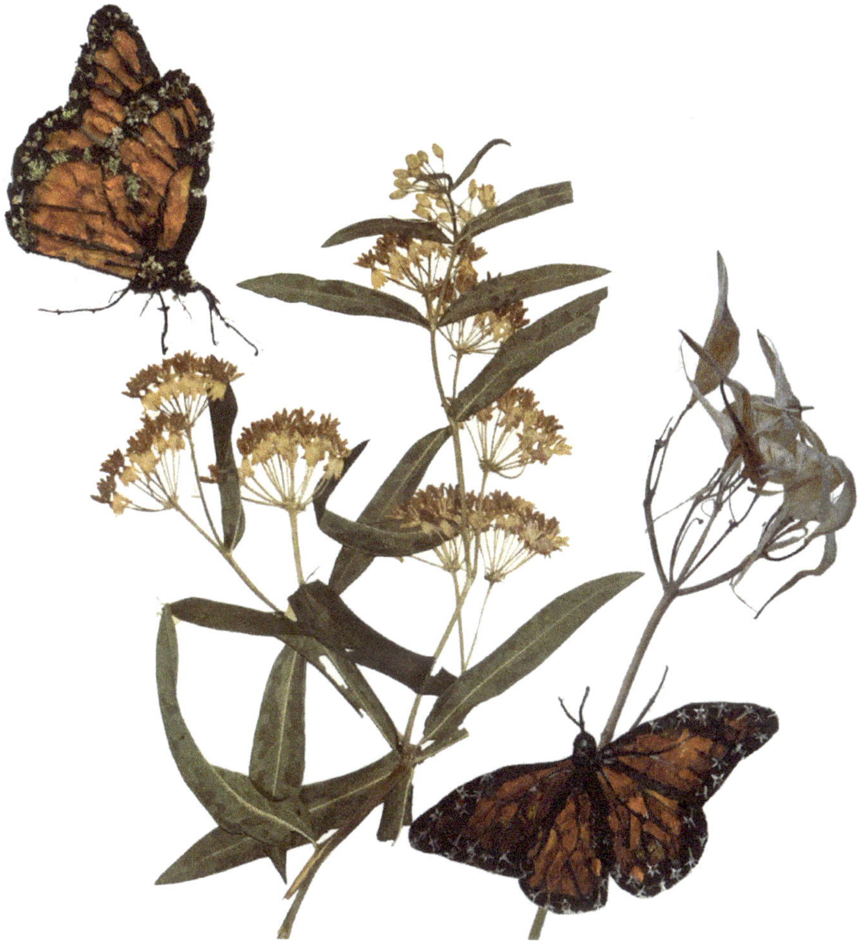

Butterfly weed - asclepias tuberosa

Swamp milkweed - asclepias incarnata

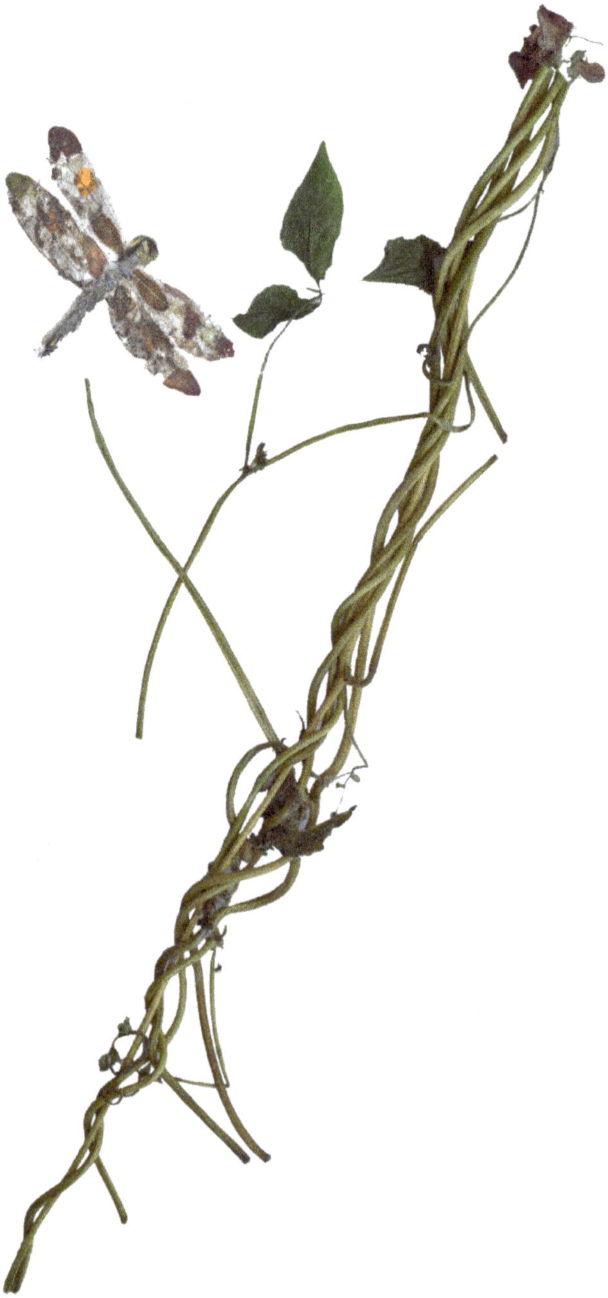

Twelve-spotted skimmer dragonfly - labella pulchella

Scarlet runner bean - phaseolus coccineus

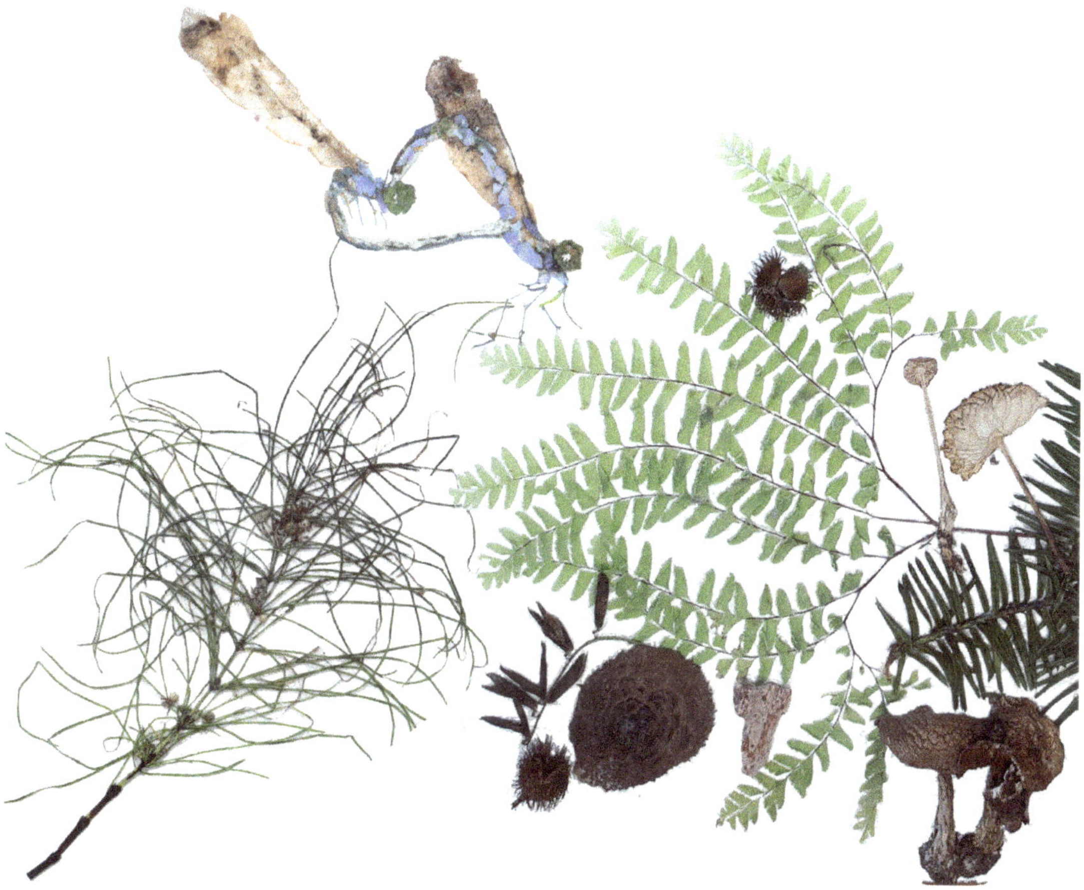

Azure bluet (damselfly)	- enallagma aspersum
Horsetail	- equisetum laevigatum
Maidenhead spleenwort	- asplenium trichomanes

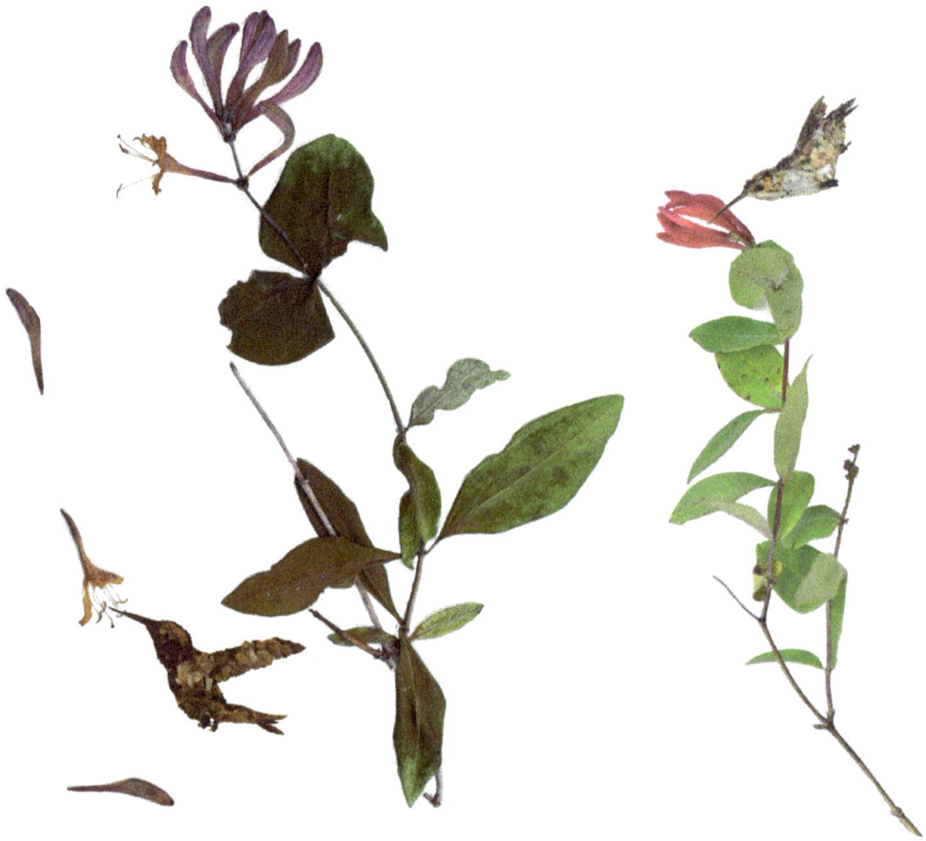

Ruby-throated hummingbird	- archilochus colubris
Honeysuckle (Trumpet)	- lonicera sempervirens

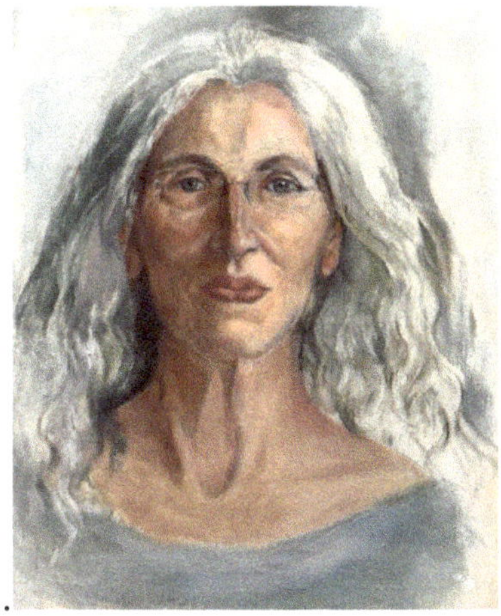 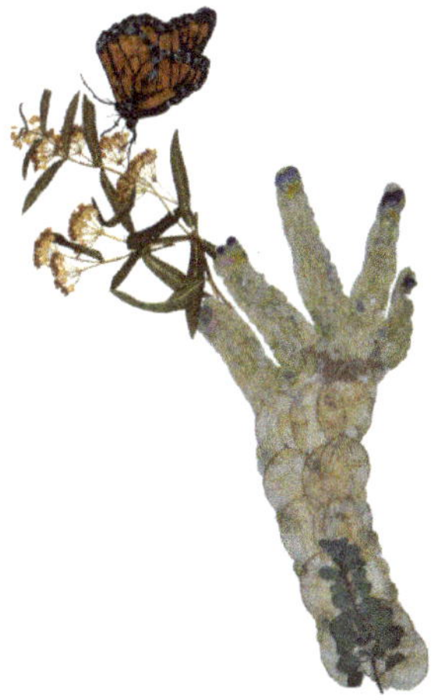

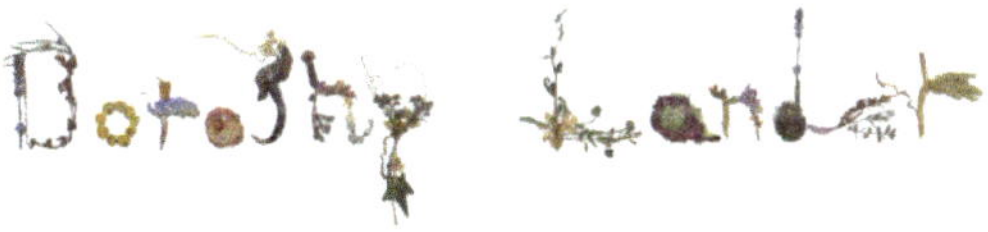

Portrait by Gillian McCulloch
Dorothy's hand and Monarch butterfly on
Asclepias tuberosa

Dorothy lives in Antigonish, Nova Scotia with her husband, John Graham-Pole where they co-founded HARP: The People's Press (www.harppublishing.ca), a multi-media publishing house dedicated to the healing arts.

Dorothy's two careers at St. Francis Xavier University (StFX), first in Operations Management and then on Adult Education faculty informs her "retirement" career as a writer and co-publisher of HARP.

Dorothy can be found on Facebook, Linked-In, and Twitter.

Experiential Responses to Hmmm – M the Humdinger

A HARP innovation, our "blurb" section unfolds with conventional by-request testimonials but with a twist —they highlight the felt experience of the reviewers and position botany and humming scholars alongside a wide diversity of general readers and listeners. Our reviewers range in age from 4 to 84. I was interested in how the story made everyone feel, and if they were reminded of their own humming practice and relationship with Nature. The responses did not disappoint and accordingly, the reviews hold considerable educational value in their own right, offering insights from children and inter-generational readers, botany creatives (artists, writers and illustrators), art-for-health practitioners, musicians and musicologists, and finally an evolutionary anthropologist and her cat.

Children and Intergenerational Readers

This delightful book is fun for all ages – my 4- year-old grand-daughter watched and listened all the way through and then went dancing and humming around the house. As this book is being published, we are in tough times. This little story reminds us that we are all special and inspires us with both the beauty of nature in the artwork and the beauty of the human voice. As we preserve art, music, and especially beauty, humans will become a less destructive species.

- Marilyn Manzer, music educator, Wolfville, Nova Scotia
  https://youtu.be/bwjYJHsWluk

It was nice to be read to for a change as it's usually me doing all the reading around here. I'm happy that it was shared with us.

- Kamila Nasr

***

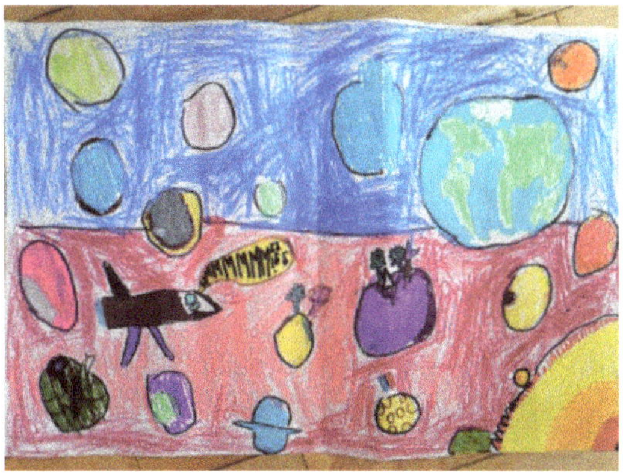

The book is about why M keeps humming, because she belongs to nature, then M becomes harmony and humming to the world.

- Ethan, age 7,Antigonish, Nova Scotia

His mom Cathy Lin reported that Ethan said he loves the artwork and he was trying to find the characters [the hummers] in each artwork.

***

I think this is a book about flowers, beautifully pressed flowers in rich vibrant colours and wonderful textures. I was totally taken with them, knowing that the time of year made me both fixate on and luxuriate in them, all the while listening to the story. Thinking I had missed a great deal the first time round, I went back to hear the story again and sure enough, the flowers drew me again. I wanted to touch the pansies, in particular, to feel their silky softness and to see how the drying process had affected them. Pansies are the true jewels of the flower world, coming out as they do when we are most in need, in late winter and early spring. The leaves, the bees, the blooms, the vines, they were magnificent for a late March day.

I found myself impatiently waiting for the time to change the page, so I could see more flowers. They are exquisite and the true medicine of this book, definitely alternative and definitely useful, though I know you have a healing story here about a gifted girl, considered to be ill, and a wise woman who acknowledges her gifts. The flowers lifted my soul.

- Anonymous, Antigonish, Nova Scotia

Dorothy's Kin

Dorothy drew in her family to review Hmmm to assess its potential for intergenerational readers, especially for families sheltering in place during COVID. Her grand nieces and nephews among her toughest critics, and ranging in age from 7 to 16, represent the appeal of Hmmm to different age demographics, and also how reviewers can take up opposing positions. For example, Mina age 16 recommends that the images be more reflective of the storyline. Mara age 10 offers that the creative pictures really give you an understanding of what the story is trying to tell you.
***

Thanks for sharing this book with us! Miles and I read it together. I thought the storyline was pretty original and cool. I find that the kids I babysit for understand and enjoy the story more when the pictures are more reflective of the storyline. However, I did really like the touch of how the humming parts were in a different font and color.

- Mina, age 16

I think this book is for an age bracket that I am no longer in. I think that younger kids may like the book, but it wasn't my kinda read.

- Miles, age 13

I liked the Wise Woman and how she used the Honeysuckle bush to connect M with the hummingbirds and bees. Also, the moss covered stone in the forest seemed like the one at Tower Farm. [the Lander family farm]

- Tannen, age 8

We both thought it was well done with a great message!

- Tannen and his dad Ben Lander, Teacher/Coach,White Oaks S. S., Oakville, Ontario

I gave this book 3 stars, because I thought that the story had a good meaning, that everyone is different. I loved the creative pictures throughout the book, I feel they really give you an understanding of what the story is trying to tell you. I didn't give it 5 stars is because I thought that if the book is meant for kids, I think there should be a little less information about the doctors.

I think that this is an outstanding book and includes real life events (like the doctors) in a fictional book. I would say the book is for 7-8 year olds. This is an outstanding book and I would definitely read it again.

- Mara, age 10

I liked the story because it is for kids. I liked how the story had a good message in the end about M, that it is ok to be different.

- Kate, age 7

Hmmm takes you on a beautifully mysterious magical journey. Although Hmmm is categorized as a children's book, it is a story for any age. The flip book is accompanied with sound. This includes a reading of the text and various humming melodies that express M's feelings. You could also read and hum your own melodies to experience M's unique communication abilities.

In this way we join M on her journey as her loved ones attempt to make sense of her humming and possibly even fix it. M hums through her encounters with curiosity, grace, and certainty. We come to understand that M's humming is her gift.

This is a story which fills you with wonder and whimsy as you hum along with M's message of acceptance. It's a story which both delights and soothes while it offers an important message about the meaning of difference.

- Susan Napier, stepdaughter, social worker, artist, L'Arche service worker, Antigonish, Nova Scotia

Children are especially interested in bees these days - the world depends on pollinators. Lots of butterflies, birds, bees and flowers here. The girl M in the story is examined to see why she keeps humming - simple medical opinions.

- June Bowman, sister, grandmother, aunt, library volunteer, Cobourg, Ontario

***

A truly heart-warming, educational tale of M's quest to find out what was different about her — but she actually discovers that her humming is a very special gift. The illustrations are amazing and so harmonious with nature!

- Brenda Manley, (Dorothy's childhood friend) Retired Teacher SS # 16, Grandmother, Children's Choir Director, Port Hope, Ontario

<u>Botany Creatives: Writers and Illustrators</u>

I have never come across anything quite like this before. It is illustrated with the most wonderful plant collages, I especially love the ones at the back of the book where the plants and insects are named. The best thing of all is the therapeutic benefit of humming along. This would be a great book to read alongside a younger reader, you would certainly have plenty of fun along the way.

- Rachel Corby, Plant Whisperer, Personal Rewilding Coach, author of Rewilding & The Art Of Plant Whispering.

Hmmm; how to sing the praises this wonderful book? Simply by humming! As I turned the pages of this story, delighting in its gentle narrative and playful, pressed flower illustrations, I began to hum, deeply and contentedly. So much so that it tickled my heart! Indeed, so much so, I reread it, over and over again! A beautiful story for young and old, especially those who, like me, over the years have somewhat neglected their hummm!

- Jane Hall, artist and author of The Art of Embroidered Butterflies @clothofnature http://clothofnature.com/

***

Hmmm: M the Humdinger by Dorothy Lander tells the story of a child who communicates by humming.

It begins with fascinating facts about the value of humming, including examples of the range of emotions that humming can convey, its deep history and healing properties. This is followed by a humming primer to help us as we're encouraged to hum along with the humming parts in the ensuing story.

The story encompasses a wealth of information, from medical specialties to such obscure items of interest as the clockwise twining of honeysuckle versus the counter clockwise twining of bindweed. The text is accompanied by complex images of pressed flowers and insects.

- Celia Godkin, author and illustrator, www.celiagodkin.com

***

Hmmm is a bedtime story and a delightful sensual experience. My warm congratulations! There were so many things I loved about it (sibilant/siblings, the complexity and colouring of the drawings, the quality of the story, and more).

- Rachel McAlpine, writer, poet, drawer, blogger, and podcast host, author of romance novel Humming. https://writeintolife.com Wellington, New Zealand

Art-for-Health Practitioners
For Dorothy and M

As I read the Primer I tried humming myself to see if it might be something I've forgotten how to do. I found that not only can I hum... I actually make little humming sounds all the time... when I'm deeply touched by something someone says or when I read something that resonates with me.

I'm a nurse and I kept thinking about M's mom and dad and their trips to all of the specialists... and how we (in healthcare) always start a file. It moved M to the role of pediatric patient. They are such good parents to try to better understand their little daughter. Although they are trying to protect her, I kept hoping they would celebrate her more... instead of trying to see what was wrong and in need of fixing ... to name and champion her special and magnificent gift. Saying this ... I did love the Wise Woman. She held the space and saw the gift! Each of us needs a Wise Woman. As I think about it, I hope (humbly) that to someone else, I might be their Wise Woman... that I hold the space for them and that I see their gifts... and that I name them.

I felt a little sadness at the end because M turned into a natural sound (although beautiful). I wanted her to be more. I wanted her to teach others to hum and to celebrate being gifted. I suspect that if I read the book many times... knowing the ending, that I would not feel this sadness... I would celebrate that she was a gift of nature in human-form for a brief while.

This is a book I would have loved to read (and hum) to my children and my grandchildren.

- Barb Heatley O'Neil, BScN, M.Ad.Ed., CPCC
  President: O'Neil Co-Active Coaching Group, Nurse
  Leader and Wise Woman, Sarnia, Ontario

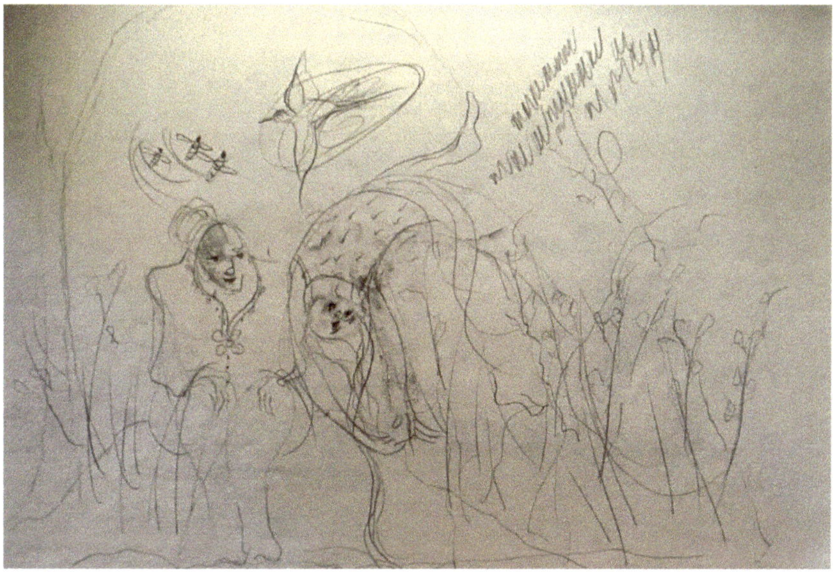

A quick sketch inspired by M. – Gail Butters Cohen

Gail and Dorothy were both part of the all-woman cohort of the three-week Arts and Health Summer Intensive at the Center for Arts in Medicine at the University of Florida in 2005.
https://arts.ufl.edu/academics/center-for-arts-in-medicine/programs/professional-development-internships/uf-gainesville/

Within the pages of this wondrous, musical tale of M. I was instantly uplifted, elegantly swished and swirled into flight and fancy. Curiosity and mystery held me captivated as I found myself joyfully creeping and crawling, flitting and flying on colorful wings, amongst the beauty and forget me not botanicals, the marvels of Nature's splendor. The wildflowers reverberated and danced across the colorful, decorative pages, carrying me beyond the meadows and deep into the magical vibrations of M's mysterious, intuitive gift.

Thank you for allowing me to read...yes, the wise woman spoke to me...a woman I have yearned to meet the entirety of my life-time but have not as of yet...the woman who would "know" and recognize the "me" I have longed to be ... just as she KNEW Your beloved M!

- Gail Butters Cohen, Freelance Artist and Illustrator, Early Childhood Educator, Creative Arts Facilitator, West Palm Beach, Florida Website: https://gail-cohen.pixels.com/ Facebook: https://www.facebook.com/groups/Creative-HeARThsHealing/

***

Musicians and Musicologists

I was delighted to hear so many aspects of humming, one of the most neglected and at the same time, one of the crucially important for all human being's vocal activities, woven into the story so ably!

Introducing this story to our small listeners can have profound importance to them, as humming comes from unimaginable depths of our evolutionary prehistory, originating millions of years earlier than our speech. Deeper evolutionary roots naturally mean a more effective connection to human emotional life. Humming can do magics in creating emotions, transferring emotions to others, connecting us to nature. And all this natural wisdom is presented wrapped in a delightfully engaging story. I am impressed!

- Joseph Jordania, ethnomusicologist and evolutionary musicologist. Honorary Fellow Melbourne Conservatorium of Music, University of Melbourne, Australia

The Humdinger is a fascinating and well-written work. I have read your book with such enthusiasm.

It is no less than the summation of the artistic intelligence and experience of the human's humming voice epitomized as a symbol of good health.

The Humdinger captures music's transformative ability and illustrates the connections of humming to wellness all-around from the cell, sub-cellular to molecular levels of our biological existence.

- Dr. David O. Akombo, professor of music, and author of The Unity of Music and Dance in World Cultures. Jackson, Mississippi

***

The book is exquisite. The illustrations are beautiful.
I like the idea of humming. It has the advantage you do not have to remember any words.

- Dr. Roger Boston, M.D., Family physician, concert violinist, Tbilisi, Georgia

Evolutionary Anthropologist

Hmmm is like no other book, in several ways. First of all, its story is as "different" as its heroine, whose name is M. Unlike you and me, she does not talk. Instead, like nature's hummers—bees, dragonflies, and hummingbirds—she hums, beautifully and musically.

Additionally, Hmmm is a book of sounds, not only words and beautiful pictures. It is not only multimedia, but "multigenerational" – a story that will appeal to adults and youngsters alike, and to anyone who loves music, poetry, and the wonders of nature.

Hmmm is an innovative and original contribution to the fields of arts-in-healthcare and music therapy. Its gorgeous floral pictures and beautiful sounds put the findings of arts-in-healthcare into practice.

M's experiences make clear that most people today live in "vocal deserts." Humming, like music and immersion in nature, are good for us. They heal.

- Ellen Dissanayake is the author of What Is Art For?, Homo Aestheticus: Where Art Comes From and Why, and Art and Intimacy: How the Arts Began, all published by the University of Washington Press, Seattle.

As I was listening to p. 8 on the computer in my bedroom, my cat, who had been sleeping in the living room, came in and jumped up on the desk beside me (as she often does). She heard a hmmmmmm and immediately became alert and looked at the screen with interest, then outside the window behind it. As other Mmmmms sounded, she got up and looked behind the computer. Throughout the story, whenever there were longish stretches of, to her, boring people-language, she lay down and went back to her usual thoughts. But when the various Mmmmms began again, she always showed interest and looked at the screen.

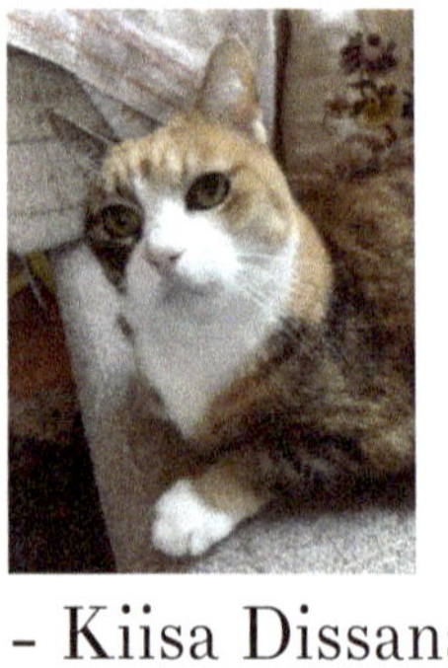

- Kiisa Dissanayake, Seattle, Washington, USA

www.ingramcontent.com/pod-product-compliance
Ingram Content Group UK Ltd.
Pitfield, Milton Keynes, MK11 3LW, UK
UKHW060125010826
14089UKWH00006B/162

9 780993 829574